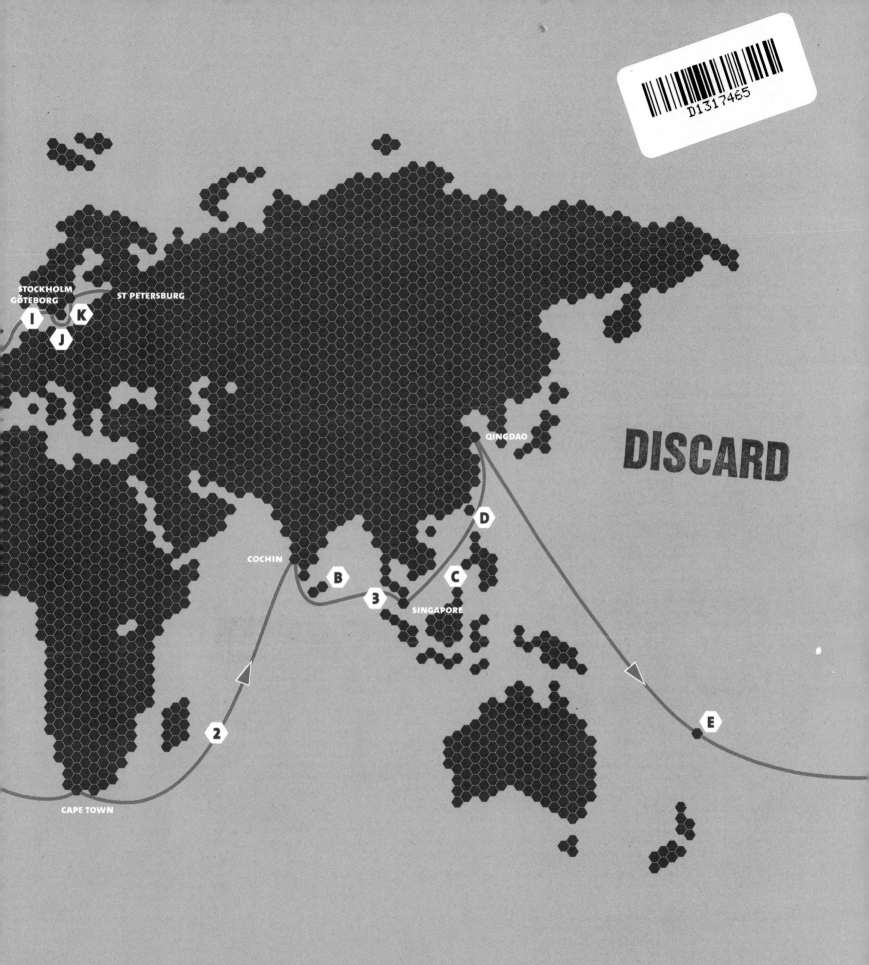

STOCKHOLM
GÖTEBORG
ST PETERSBURG

QINGDAO

DISCARD

COCHIN

B

C

D

SINGAPORE

CAPE TOWN

2

3

E

I

J

K

dakini
media

a dakini book

Spanish Castle to White Night

The Race Around the World

Mark Chisnell

First published in 2009
Copyright © dakini Media Ltd

dakini is an award-winning and innovative London-based publisher specialising in books of exceptional quality on sport, the environment, popular culture and design.

Publisher Lucky Dissanayake
Author Mark Chisnell
Editor Richenda Todd
Project manager dakini Jo Grummitt
Project assistant dakini Gemma Grass-Orkin
Project manager Volvo Ocean Race Lizzie Ward
Picture editor Tim Stonton
Design Anikst Design, London
Front cover design Cradduck Design
Prepress Richard Deal, Dexter Pre-media
Editorial advisor Barthold A. van Doorn

T: +44 (0)20 7830 9692
F: +44 (0)20 7830 9693
www.dakinibooks.com

ISBN: 978-0-9552615-2-7

A CIP catalogue record of this book is available from the British Library
Printed and bound in Italy by L. O. C. E. Srl in Stige Spa

A note from the author

There are lots of people involved in a project like this, and although my name is on the cover it would never have happened without the contributions of many others. It is not possible to do this individually as so many people were involved, but I would like to say a big thank you to everyone at the Volvo Ocean Race, at dakini Media, the team press officers, media crew members and, of course, Frances Clarke, who worked hard with me on early drafts of the text.

I would also like to thank the individual crewmen without whom this book would not have been possible. Each of them told me their stories as well as they were able, sometimes weeks later on the longer legs. And while I have retold them as entertainingly and as accurately as possible the memory is a fragile thing (certainly where something as complex as sailboat racing is concerned), and I'm sure that some will have different recollections.

However big this book, it was always going to be impossible to tell all the stories that came out of this race, and I'm sorry that there wasn't more space for those other recollectios and other tales. I have tried hard to distill the essence of nine months of the Volvo Ocean Race 2008–09 into the pages you find here, but the rest will have to wait for another book, another time.

And finally, I'd like to thank my family for putting up with my absence for the time it took to write this book.

Mark Chisnell
Hamble, August 2009

Photo Credits

Sergey Bogdanov/Team Russia
  68, 69, 72
Guo Chuan/Green Dragon Racing
  5, 31, 56, 70, 73, 102, 103, 106, 137, 139 (bottom), 152, 155 (bottom), 172 (top / middle bottom), 176, 178, 182, 192
Sally Collison/PUMA Ocean Racing
  49, 51 (top), 121, 174
Mark Covell/Team Russia
  19, 27, 61, 65 (top)
Rick Deppe/PUMA Ocean Racing
  40, 55, 75, 95, 116, 117, 132, 135 (bottom), 144, 181, 194
Ryan Godfrey/Ericsson 4
  126
Oskar Kihlborg/Ericsson Racing Team
  8, 12, 13
Jerry Kirby/PUMA Ocean Racing
  51 (bottom)
Dave Kneale/Volvo Ocean Race
  14 (bottom), 17, 32, 33, 36 (bottom), 66 (bottom), 84, 85, 90, 108, 112, 113, 115, 162, 163, 169, 184, 185, 186, 187, 188, 204, 207, 212
Gustav Morin/Ericsson 3
  52, 53, 62, 81 (top), 86, 98, 109, 135 (top), 147, 172 (bottom), 191 (left)
Maria Muina/Equipo Telefónica
  14 (top)
EricNorth.co.uk/BotinCarkeek.com
  228, 229
Gabriele Olivo/Telefónica Blue
  65 (bottom), 79, 97 (top), 99, 123, 128, 129, 143, 148, 155 (top)
Mikel Pasabant/Telefónica Black
  97 (bottom)
Sander Pluijm/Team Delta Lloyd
  2, 3, 28, 29, 81 (bottom), 83, 100, 105, 170, 172 (middle top), 191 (right)
Guy Salter/Ericsson 4
  9, 76, 118, 139 (top), 208
Swedish Coast Guard
  220, 221
Rick Tomlinson/Volvo Ocean Race
  6, 7, 11, 24, 35, 36 (top), 39, 42, 43, 44, 45, 46, 48, 58, 59, 66 (top), 88, 89, 92, 93, 110, 111, 125, 156, 158, 159, 160, 165, 166, 168, 198, 200, 201, 202, 203, 211, 214, 215, 216, 219, 224, 225, 240
Volvo Ocean Race
  22, 150, 197
Matthias Witzany
  20, 21
Jiang Yongtao
  222

Rick Tomlinson/Volvo Ocean Race
  Front cover image
Gabriele Olivo/Telefónica Blue
  Back cover image

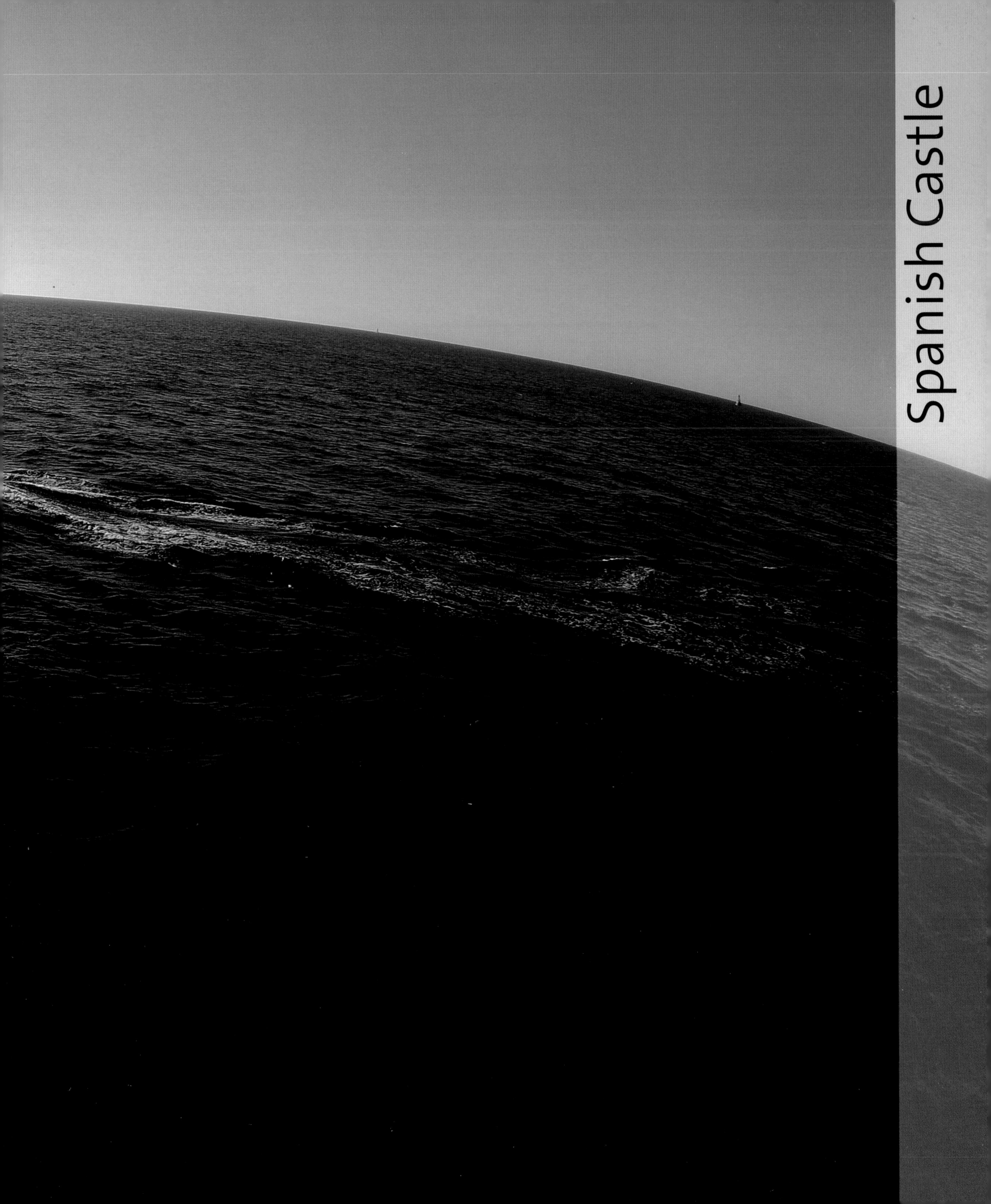
Spanish Castle

chapter opener PUMA and the wide blue yonder.

left Ericsson 4 at full power, sailing downwind with an asymmetric spinnaker. On leg one, this boat and crew broke the world 24-hour record, setting a new mark at 596.6 nautical miles — beating the old record by just over 33 nautical miles, but falling short of the magic 600 miles in 24 hours.

right Stu Bannatyne, one of Ericsson 4's two watch captains, at the wheel. Each crew is split into two watches, one of which is up on deck sailing the boat while the other is normally resting below. Although the skipper has overall control, the watch captains take much of the responsibility for the speed and sailing of the boat.

By the early afternoon of 29 October 2008, the racing yacht Ericsson 4 had been on world-record pace for almost 36 hours. Fourteen tonnes of Volvo Open 70 in a relentless charge across the South Atlantic, driven by 35 knots of wind pressing on hundreds of square metres of high-technology fabric.

They had first punched through the old mark — 562.96 nautical miles in a day — in the early hours of the morning. The mileage eased briefly after breakfast, but then it clicked relentlessly upwards once again. Now they were closing on a new barrier — 600 miles in a day, sailing at an average 25 knots; that meant 25 nautical miles for each and every one of the 24 hours. This was new territory.

At the wheel just after midday was Stu Bannatyne, the watch captain. He had held the same position aboard the 2001–02 Volvo Ocean Race winner, illbruck. Bannatyne is softly spoken. On first meeting, you might think him shy, or aloof. Not at all the kind of a man you imagine flying through freezing southern oceans at maniacal speeds, with the lives of everyone on board in his hands. But the quiet reserve hides iron resolve and a single-minded focus: useful qualities when the slightest hesitation can spell disaster.

Bannatyne's first trip away from his native New Zealand was to the 1989 ISAF World Youth Championships in Canada. It wasn't so different from home, though there was plenty to distract a curious teenager on his first trip abroad. But none of it had any effect on Bannatyne, who came away with the Single-handed World Championship. In doing so he joined a pantheon of sailing luminaries that includes triple Olympic gold medallist Ben Ainslie, and three-time America's Cup winner Russell Coutts.

Now Stu Bannatyne was applying all that focus, constantly bracing every nerve and muscle against the elemental battering. The elevated helming position provided a great view in daylight, but left him exposed to everything that the ocean could hurl at the boat. Protection was afforded by a survival suit, a windsurfing helmet with a full face visor, and he was tethered to a strong line, the jackstay, that runs transversely across the boat by the wheels.

There were just three men on deck with him: two on the sheets, and one at the double-handed winch pedestal, grinding the sails in response to the commands. Those commands were the only words spoken; the howl of wind and waves and the screech of winches allowed for nothing else. This was sailing at the very edge of human endeavour, and they all knew it.

They were sailing the boat at the fastest possible angle to the wind. Now, the wind shifted slightly, forcing them into the waves. Instead of skipping across the back of each one at a steady 26 or 27 knots, Bannatyne was forced to sail down the face, which accelerated them to a speed that would have earned him a fine in an urban area, not to mention the opprobrium of his wife, Amanda. Then the boat ploughed itself into the back of the wave in front, plunging the foredeck into green water and washing a white wall of boiling foam and spray back down the boat.

If the motion was bad before, now it was impossible. Down below, men were trying to follow the normal routines of any other day: eat, sleep, wash, dress. But this was not a normal day — this might be a day that people would talk about for years to come, the day when Ericsson 4 went through the 600-mile barrier. And then there was a bang.

right   The Volvo Ocean Race fleet prepares to leave the dock in Alicante for the in-port racing. It comprised a day of one or more races over a short course; these events were first introduced in the 2005–06 edition. They accounted for 20 per cent of the overall points, and were held in seven of the 11 ports visited in 2008–09.

overleaf   The Ericsson team began preparations early, after a disappointing performance by the single boat that raced in their colours in 2005–06. They hired the winning designer from the previous race and committed to a two-boat team. That allowed for long months of training and testing from their base in the Canary Islands – the benefit of which was immediately obvious at the start of leg one.

Eighteen days earlier, eight Volvo Open 70s had left the Race Village in Alicante to the cheers of tens of thousands of spectators. They had started the first leg of the 2008–09 Volvo Ocean Race, bound for Cape Town, South Africa, on a grim, grey day. The wind was blowing hard out of the northeast – more North Sea winter than Mediterranean autumn. The fleet sailed a lap of the bay in sight of the tenth-century Castle of Santa Bárbara, before turning southwest towards the Cabo de Palos, the first of two capes they would have to negotiate on their way to the Straits of Gibraltar, and then the Atlantic.

No one was particularly surprised when Ericsson 4 led the way down the coast. They came to the race with impeccable credentials, part of a two-boat operation, with sister ship Ericsson 3 also racing. The group behind the team had been involved with the race since the 1980s. They won it with Team EF in 1997–98, were second in 2001–02, but in the previous race had slipped to fifth, with Ericsson as a sponsor.

The giant communications technology company was eager for another go. This time they started early, with the designer of the winning boat from the last race, the Argentinian Juan Kouyoumdjian. They hired a world-class crew, led by Brazilian Torben Grael, who has an enviable collection of Olympic medals (two gold, two bronze and a silver), as well as having led a Brazilian team to third place in the previous race.

They weren't the only ones with a score to settle. Telefónica Blue and Telefónica Black were the second of the race's two-boat teams. Led by five-time Volvo veteran Bouwe Bekking – sports and technical director

as well as skipper of the Blue boat – their ill-starred 2005–06 Volvo Ocean Race had opened with a first-night structural problem which forced them to retire from leg one. A tragic conclusion was narrowly avoided when their yacht, movistar, had finally been abandoned in the Atlantic Ocean on leg seven, after the keel structure had suffered a dangerous failure.

Jonathan Swain, who had climbed into the liferaft with Bekking on that occasion, was back as watch captain aboard Telefónica Blue for 2008–09. They were just a couple of hours out from Alicante when Swain took the wheel. They had a small spinnaker up and a reef in; conditions were fresh, but not frightening – as the saying would have it. But almost immediately Swain lost control of the boat, rounding up into the wind – broaching, sails flapping. He heaved on the wheel and got her back on track, only to lose it again. Bekking frowned; his instructions to Swain had been to take it easy. They needed to settle into the race before pushing hard.

Something wasn't right, and it didn't take long to find the problem. The tiller arm – the strut that connects the rudder to the steering gear and the wheels on deck – was broken. The starboard rudder was flapping uselessly. They had limited control with the port rudder, which was fine when the boat was upright. But when Telefónica Blue heeled over on to her starboard side, the good rudder came out of the water and they quickly lost control. Fortunately, once they were past Cabo de Palos they had the option to sail back towards the coast. That put the working rudder in the water, and also got them into calmer conditions, so they could work on the repair.

They dug the boatbuilding spares out of the bag – not something they had imagined doing so soon after

the start. It seemed as if Bekking and Swain's first-night jinx had struck again. But this was a great deal less serious than the problems of 2005, and five hours later – although they weren't convinced of the durability of the repair – they had full control of the boat.

The tiller arms had been a problem earlier in their preparation, so two brand-new, redesigned units had been delivered to their facility in Alicante. But, because they were an unknown quantity, they had decided not to fit them before the start. Now that decision had come back to haunt them. They could call into a port and swap them, but that meant taking a 12-hour penalty – the minimum time a team was allowed to suspend racing to seek help.

Bouwe Bekking and navigator Simon Fisher pored over the charts and weather maps to find the most efficient spot, and chose the Bay of Gibraltar. Decision made, they pulled into Algeciras on the evening of Sunday 12 October. Their support crew met them with a van full of equipment, and sent the sailors to a local hotel. Swain reflected afterwards that it had been a strange sensation – lying in a comfortable bed, hours after they should have left shore-side comforts behind for the three-week race to South Africa.

In Swain's case, the journey was a kind of homecoming. Brought up in Durban, on South Africa's east coast, Swain was born to English parents, not long after they emigrated to their new home. He has subsequently proved no less prone to wanderlust himself, and now lives in Florida, with his American wife Cary, and their two children. He stuck around in South Africa just long enough to get an education and

top **Telefónica Black chases Telefónica Blue** downwind at the Copa del Rey, a big Spanish regatta in Palma de Mallorca in the summer of 2008. The team had their base in Alicante. Unfortunately, Telefónica Black was only built in time for a couple of months of two-boat training before the race started.

bottom left **Telefónica Blue** ties up in Algeciras harbour. She met her shore crew to replace a tiller arm that broke just hours after the start of leg one. Although it was initially repaired on the water, because it was an important component of the steering system, the crew elected to change it for a completely new unit.

bottom right **Telefónica Blue's** shore crew removes the rudder during the replacement of the broken tiller arm. Although the repair was straightforward, the rules enforce a minimum stop (suspension of racing) of 12 hours if the crew has assistance from anyone or anything outside the boat.

It was a tough hurdle to overcome at the start of a very long race, but ultimately a good decision given the wild conditions the crew subsequently encountered en route to Cape Town.

complete his compulsory military service, and then
headed for the States, where friends had told him he
could earn a living as a sailor. And they were right.
Starting from nothing, Swain had risen to the very top
of the sport.

By 7 am the crew was back at the dock, where the
support team was giving the boat a final clean, ready to
go. They motored out to where they had suspended
racing and, exactly 12 hours later, pulled up the sails and
set off in pursuit of Ericsson 4, who led the fleet over 100
miles away.

It had been rather different a week earlier.
Telefónica Blue topped the podium in the opening
in-port racing with a brilliant performance. In the light
winds they were "unstoppable on all points of sailing",
as Swain put it afterwards. But this was a marathon,
not a 100-metre sprint. And Bouwe Bekking made it
clear to the team that even after that triumph there
should be no question of complacency. In short order,
they had reaped both the advantages and
disadvantages of having their training base in Alicante.
Dominant in the local conditions, they lacked the time
spent sailing in the stronger winds and waves more
common in the Atlantic, which might have led them to
fix the tiller-arm problem before the race started.

It had all been very different indeed almost four decades
previously, when Colonel Bill Whitbread and Admiral
Otto Steiner RNSA (Royal Naval Sailing Association) had
had their idea of a crewed yacht race round the world. It
certainly hadn't included in-port racing. But like many
good ideas, it had its genesis in a pub – the Still and
West on Portsmouth waterfront where, legend has it,

the pair brewed up the notion of the race. It was a
different world back then. A dozen men had just walked
on the moon, but not many more had sailed a yacht
successfully through the Southern Ocean and round
Cape Horn. Steiner and Whitbread proposed a fully
crewed race through those same waters.

Seventeen yachts accepted the challenge and
turned up at HMS Vernon, a Portsmouth naval base, in
the autumn of 1973. The genesis of the modern Race
Village was just an encampment of pay phones,
sailmakers tents and caravans selling yacht gear. The
boats were loaded with fresh food, wine, real bunks and
dining tables. They were mostly privately owned or
entered by the armed forces, and the crews were largely
amateur. Setting a trend, some were more ready than
others. Burton Cutter was still being built as she crossed
the start line. Fourteen boats finished, but three men
died: Paul Waterhouse went overboard from Tauranga,
Dominique Guillet from 33 Export and Bernie Hosking
from Chay Blyth's Great Britain II. Questions were asked:
Was this sport? But, at the prize-giving, the organisers
announced that the race would be run again in four
years' time.

Two years later a rival round-the-world race was
held, with a single stop in Sydney and sponsorship from
the Financial Times. Only four boats competed and the
exercise was not repeated. In contrast, 15 yachts came to
the line for the second Whitbread Race in 1977. A classic
was born, and then nurtured. But 25 years and seven
races after they began, Whitbread finally decided that
they had had enough.

It was the Swedish industrial giant Volvo that
stepped in to pick up the mantle of the world's

top   A crewman is hauled aloft aboard Team Russia. It's usually the bowman who goes up the mast. He is pulled up on one of the halyards, using the winches that would normally raise the sails. The rig needs to be regularly checked for chafe and any sign of cracks or damage, and sometimes the halyards get twisted in sail changes and need to be freed. The tip of the mast is over 31 metres above the water, so the job of going up there is a lot less popular when it's rough.

bottom   Jeremy Elliott works at the sewing machine down below on Team Russia. The yachts can carry up to 13 sails and each sail is used in a specific range of wind speeds and angles to the wind. If any sail is damaged then its replacement will not perform as well in those conditions, so it's really important for the crews to be able to repair damage at sea.

greatest crewed round-the-world race. And more changes followed to an event that had constantly evolved in boat design, format and route. The 2008–09 Volvo Ocean Race was the third iteration, and the second to involve the crash and burn of in-port racing (literally in this case: two boats collided on the start line in Alicante). But while the in-port action accounted for 20 per cent of the available points, the heart and soul of the Volvo Ocean Race remained in the name: ocean racing.

Telefónica Blue wasn't the only one with problems, now that the teams were finally at sea. Team Russia was an unusual entry among its corporate brethren. In a Race Village overwhelmed by the displays, exhibitions and pageants of modern brand communications, Team Russia sat bereft of all slogans and logos save one: 'Team Russia sails for the whale', actively supporting the message of the Whale and Dolphin Conservation Society.

St Petersburg businessman Oleg Zherebtsov wanted to do the Volvo Ocean Race, and he wanted to do it for the right reasons. So he asked Andreas Hanakamp to skipper a campaign for him, and together they set up a team, built a boat, chose a cause, and then Zherebtsov planned to take his place aboard, working at the sharp end, on the foredeck. But just days before the start in Alicante, Zherebtsov had to return to Russia after the tragic death of his mother.

The team set off without him. And they were soon in trouble. Before the start gun had even gone, they had water pouring into the boat. The keel on a Volvo Open 70 is swung (or canted) from one side to the other to provide additional leverage. The movement of several

tonnes of lead bulb on the end of a steel fin provides a highly efficient counterbalance to the pressure of the wind on the sails.

To achieve this canting effect, the keel fin pivots on giant pins inserted into the base of the hull, and above the pivot sit two massive hydraulic rams that push the top of the fin from side to side. As the pivot is not waterproof, the whole lot is surrounded by a solid carbon-fibre 'wet-box', which is sealed at the top by a transparent plate, so the crew can see inside. The two rams push on the top of the keel via holes in each side of the wet-box, and they are sealed by 'ram boots' – flexible waterproofing around the ram arms, allowing them to move. Team Russia's ram boots had cracked and were leaking badly.

They put the bilge pumps on and started bailing. But within a couple of hours it became clear that this wasn't sustainable; they didn't have the manpower to bail and sail the boat. They had to fix the leak. They started work as they settled into the run down to Cabo de Palos. Positioning the boat a little to leeward of the fleet, they got caught in a squall with more breeze and the wind direction shifting against them. Trying to hold on to the wrong sail until they clawed around the cape, they blew it into pieces.

Wrestling the wreckage down below, sailmaker and trimmer Jeremy Elliott could have been forgiven for cursing the kind of upbringing that had cemented an unbreakable affiliation with boats and the ocean. He had been brought up in a house that overlooked the water in the southwest Irish harbour town of Kinsale. Everybody sailed there. In 1985, when Elliott was six, pop star Simon Le Bon's Whitbread Maxi, Drum, turned up in

right Team Russia sails upwind; the keel has been 'canted' so the fin and bulb are completely clear of the water. The movement of several tonnes of lead bulb on the end of a steel fin provides a highly efficient counterbalance to the pressure of the wind on the sails. To achieve this canting effect, the keel fin pivots on giant pins inserted into the base of the hull – a mechanism that is visible in orange paint on the underside of the hull. Inside the boat, and above the pivot, sit two massive hydraulic rams, which push the top of the fin from side to side.

the harbour. It was a vivid inspiration, and the young Elliott was bitterly disappointed when he was judged too young to join his father aboard for a sail.

The fire was kept burning by the 1989–90 Irish Whitbread Race entry, NCB Ireland (lovingly nicknamed by others in the fleet "Nice Cruising Boat", or rather less kindly, "Not Coming Back"). In time, Elliott found his way into the ranks of professional sailing, and now here he was, setting off on his first Volvo Ocean Race – and responsible for fixing the mess of sail cloth. But he'd never quite got over his bouts of first-night seasickness. And as anyone who is prone to it will know, the one thing that will bring it on is working down below. Elliott faced up to 24 hours of confined labour repairing the sail.

On the upside, being a thorough, thoughtful kind of guy (with more than a passing resemblance to Harry Potter when he has his glasses on), he had gone to some trouble in his preparation for this moment. A spinnaker is shaped in the same way as a dress or a shirt. The three dimensions of the finished product are created by careful tailoring of the two-dimensional panels from which it is constructed. The hard part when rebuilding a broken sail in the mobile confines of a Volvo Open 70 hull is not, despite appearances, how to move hundreds of square metres of cloth through the jaws of a tiny sewing machine in a space smaller than the average bathroom, but how to do all that and restore the damaged panels in such a way that the sail retains its original, designed shape.

To help in this task, Elliott had worked on the principle that when any sail breaks, it rips as far as the

left A sequence (top to bottom) of Ericsson 4 crewman Tony Mutter being evacuated from the boat at the Cape Verde Islands. Mutter had a badly infected knee, and was dressed in his survival suit and life jacket to swim across to the pick-up boat. The emergency procedures put in place by both Volvo Ocean Race management and the teams are always evolving, often in tandem with the technology. They now include doctors available 24 hours a day for consultation via voice and data satellite communications, so pictures of injuries or diagrams of suggested procedures can be sent back and forth.

nearest seam, and then tears along it. When he had designed each spinnaker, he'd had the laser plotter indelibly print 'tear lines' 150 millimetres back from each edge of the panel when it was marked out and cut. This defined a panel equal in proportions to the old one, but 150 millimetres smaller in each dimension. Once the sail had been dismantled around the damage, Elliott and crewmate Ben Costello had to cut along the pre-marked tear lines on each damaged seam, and then sew the pieces back together with the tear lines all matching, which should ensure that the sail was rebuilt in the original shape.

For hours they battled away at the sail, with Elliott occasionally rushing to the hatch to throw up. Around them, others struggled to stem the flow of water into Team Russia from the leaking ram boots. And all this against the background of constant bailing, and the race to Gibraltar. Eventually, a waterproof kitbag was chopped up to provide the perfect material to stem the leak. And after 20 hours' work, the sail was finished and Elliott's sickness was gone. When they put the sail back up, it looked almost new. Elliott noted a couple of little tweaks he'd like to do when it came back down. But it stayed up, and in one piece, for the next eight days of sailing.

Those eight days took the fleet all the way down the coast of Africa, past the Canaries and the Cape Verde Islands, the pace unrelenting once they got into the trade winds. The Azores High was a lot further west than normal, and it had left a band of stronger wind on the coast. Telefónica Blue used it to get themselves back in touch with the fleet. But her sister ship, Telefónica Black, made big losses by going to the west of the Canary Islands, thus sailing out of the best of the breeze and replacing Blue in last place. The temptation to go west was understandable, not least because of the old maxim: Never let anyone get west of you entering the Doldrums. It had worked beautifully for the winner in 2005–06, but by the end of the first week at sea, everyone who had gone that way had lost ground.

The highest-profile casualty was Ericsson 4, who had led the fleet for most of the journey south, only giving up their advantage when they ventured too far west after passing the Canary Islands. Then, just after breakfast on the morning of 16 October, the team indicated to the duty officer at Race Headquarters in Whiteley, England, that they had a different kind of problem. Tasked with a 24/7 watch over the fleet by all the means that modern satellite communications allow, the duty officers are always the first stop when there is any kind of issue, big or small, aboard the boats.

Ericsson 4 informed the duty officer that New Zealander Tony Mutter had an infected knee and the crewmen (trained as on-board medics by the Ericsson team and Volvo Ocean Race management) were requesting advice. The first stop in such circumstances would normally be the race's own medical coordinator, Polly Gough. But, in a coincidence you couldn't write as fiction, she was having surgery that day, to repair damage to an injured knee.

The next stop was the on-call medical adviser at the time, Dr Spike Briggs, an anaesthetist at a hospital on the south coast of England. He requested more information, including photos and measurements of

both knees so that the swelling could be judged. Questions and answers were fired back across the satcom, and soon Briggs advised that further oral antibiotics be administered, then the inflamed wound was to be incised and drained, cleaned and dressed.

On the boat, Stu Bannatyne got ready to help with the task. Bannatyne had been the medic on several of these races, including the one he had won with illbruck in 2001–02. But this was the most serious condition that he'd seen. They photographed the procedure, and sent the pictures to Briggs for analysis. By evening, Mutter was no better, and the crew contacted the team management and asked them to look at a possible evacuation – the Cape Verde Islands were looming to the south. Wheels began to turn; the situation was constantly assessed. How bad was Mutter? What were the risks of continuing? How much time would it cost them to drop him off, and where and when could it be done to incur the least penalty?

The following morning – after another round of checks, photos and consultations – the decision was taken to evacuate Mutter to a boat coming out from São Vicente in the Cape Verde Islands. Ericsson 4 gybed off course towards the rendezvous. The rescue boat was late, and it was more than two frustrating hours after the intended meeting that they finally made contact.

Mutter slipped into the water in his survival suit, his gear in a dry bag, and into the helping hands of the Cape Verde Islanders. For Polly Gough, coming out of surgery herself, there was relief that the system had worked. There had been constant encouragement to the crews to deal with problems early, before small issues became big ones. And Ericsson 4, with the help of the Race management and their shore team, had done just that.

Tony Mutter was safe in hospital, with his own team doctor in attendance. It took several days of intravenous antibiotics before the infection was beaten, and, as Bannatyne explained afterwards, they couldn't have dealt with that on board. Mutter was in Cape Town to greet the boat, and back to full fitness for the start of the next leg. While his crewmates had lost around 50 miles to the fleet, they were still racing. With the Doldrums coming up, there was every opportunity for a return to the front row. It could hardly have been a better advertisement for how the whole emergency procedure should work.

Elsewhere, other medical issues weren't quite so dramatic. Green Dragon was another team that, like the Russians, had been put together in short order, the boat launched just a few months before the start of the race. Skipper and prime mover behind the project was Ian Walker, double Olympic silver medallist and previously skipper of the GBR Challenge at the 2003 America's Cup in Auckland. Walker had been very careful to match his project's ambitions to its resources, keeping his approach simple – and hiring some very talented people.

Amongst them was watch captain Neal McDonald, a 45-year-old Englishman who had long been one of the race's stars, taking second place as skipper of ASSA ABLOY in 2001–02, before the less successful campaign with Ericsson in 2005–06. Learning to sail in the family's Mirror dinghy and bilge-keeler from the age of five, McDonald grew up in boats and was now on his fifth Volvo Ocean Race.

left **Green Dragon closes on the scoring gate at the island of Fernando de Noronha just off the coast of Brazil after 12 days at sea. The longer legs all included points for positions at intermediate scoring gates – they were worth half those available for the whole leg.**

Nick Bubb uses the grinding pedestal aboard Team Russia to adjust the trim of the sails. The trim, or shape, of each sail is controlled by various ropes, the tension of which can subtly change the aerodynamic efficiency. But some of the loads on the ropes are very high, hence the need for winches and the grinding pedestal to turn them.

So he should have known better than to be wearing his wedding ring (he married fellow Volvo Ocean Race skipper, Lisa Charles, in 1999) aboard a sailing boat. After all, even schoolchildren are told not to wear jewellery when playing sport. Hauling sails up and down the boat in light air, McDonald grabbed the back of the raised daggerboard to get some traction, dug the ring into his finger and came away with a small cut.

The cut started to swell, and soon he couldn't get the ring off. He left it for a day hoping that the swelling would reduce, fending off help from hacksaw-wielding crewmates. In the end, he did the job himself, working a metal spike in-between the ring and the swollen flesh, and then sawing it off. Afterwards, he volunteered the information that gold isn't as soft as he'd expected.

Things were going more smoothly for the rest of the Green Dragon crew as they chased the leaders south towards the Doldrums. They had already got their fingers burned once, following Telefónica Black when they ventured west of the Canary Islands. Skipper Ian Walker and his navigator Ian Moore had realised their mistake early, and bailed out to return to the fleet, making a fraction of the losses of the Black boat. But as the Cape Verde Islands approached, they started to edge west again, and this time they committed.

The initial impact was a big loss on the leader board. McDonald noted afterwards that to get west, you had to sail almost at right angles to the course to the scoring gate at Fernando de Noronha, and if everyone else was still pointing where they wanted to go, you couldn't help but tumble down the rankings. Their hope was that it was a short-term loss for a long-term gain — and everyone on Green Dragon had bought into the plan.

Then, on 19 October, the leaders hit the Doldrums. The wind softened, and the numbers clicked downwards on the speedos. To the west, Green Dragon was still moving. The plan was working. By the afternoon of that day, McDonald and his men were through into the lead, as the oppressive heat, calms and squalls of the Doldrums gripped the fleet.

The Nordic crew aboard Ericsson 3 were not having an easy ride. They had sailed into the Straits of Gibraltar heading the fleet at the side of their sister ship. The lead had unravelled as they battled the Gibraltar currents with no wind to help them. They had dropped into the pack off the coast of Africa, but fought their way back to the front. Now it seemed as if they were stuck in a bad movie sequel, as Green Dragon flew past, snorting fire.

Becalmed, 27-year-old bowman Martin Krite wrote in an email to the Race Office: *"On board Ericsson 3, time stands still. The temperature is around 40 degrees and the boat is moving very slowly through the water. The sweat is dripping down my back and no matter how much I drink, I still feel thirsty."*

A couple of years earlier, Martin Krite had quit professional sailing to marry Emilie, have a son, William, and start a theology course at Lund University. It was supposed to be the first step down a five-year path to becoming a priest. But when, in late 2007, he heard about the Nordic Volvo Ocean Race crew, sponsored by Ericsson and with many of his friends already aboard, he couldn't resist the call of another childhood dream. The Volvo beckoned, with all its previous history as the Whitbread and a great many

left   Ed van Lierde works at a sail change aboard Delta Lloyd: the old sail is gathered as it comes down. Each sail has an optimum set of conditions for performance – a range of wind speeds and angles – and once that range is exceeded the sail must be changed for a more efficient one. Sometimes the boats don't change sails for days; at other times they can be swapping them after just a few hours, or even minutes.

right   Volvo Open 70s are among the wettest offshore racing boats: water constantly flushes across the deck when there is anything more than light wind. It means that the crew has to wear foul-weather gear on deck in all but the most benign conditions. And when it's cold and rough, only full survival suits will keep them dry and vaguely warm.

famous Swedish participants. He called the skipper, Anders Lewander, to arrange a test sail, and got the job.

Krite wrote the email 24 hours before they eventually escaped the Doldrums. It was the only thing he could think to do to ease the frustration and disappointment as boat after boat slipped past them on either side. There was nowhere to hide from the heat, off-watch or on deck; and the silence, the absence of a bow wave, said everything about the struggle to get the boat moving. Ericsson 3 dropped from second to sixth by the time the wind picked up again, with the nearest boat 180 miles ahead.

Leading Ericsson 3 and the fleet into the Doldrums had been PUMA, a single-boat campaign backed by the sportswear and lifestyle company. PUMA was skippered by Ken Read, who had steered a couple of America's Cup challengers before joining McDonald aboard the struggling Ericsson for the end of the 2005–06 Volvo Ocean Race. He enjoyed the experience so much he came back for more, and the PUMA Ocean Racing Team was the result.

Joining him as navigator was the vastly experienced Andrew Cape. The pair had sailed together aboard Ericsson in the previous race, after Cape had abandoned movistar for the liferaft (with Bouwe Bekking and Jonathan Swain, now aboard Telefónica Blue), and found himself available for the final couple of legs. When Read and Cape saw the impact of Green Dragon's move they decided to cut their losses. Along with Ericsson 4, they gybed to starboard to get further west, and followed the Dragon's trail through the Doldrums. But it's tough, watching your lead get burned up, and then having to gybe and sail behind the boat that's just taken it from you.

Delta Lloyd was the eighth and final entry into the 2008–09 Volvo Ocean Race, their participation in doubt until just weeks beforehand. But they brought to the start line the winner of the previous race, ABN AMRO ONE, the only boat of that generation reckoned to have a chance against the new fleet. An Irish businessman, Ger O'Rourke, was behind the team, receiving the support from Delta Lloyd at very short notice, and leading the boat as skipper on the first leg.

The crew also came together late, with little opportunity to practise or prepare. In the light winds of the Doldrums, they levered the jumper, one of the support struts, off the mast in the dark. But with every cloud comes a silver lining. Rigger Martin Watts was subsequently presented with the Wallenius Wilhelmsen Logistics Seamanship Award for effecting a remarkable repair that kept the mast in the boat all the way to Cape Town. Nevertheless, it would hinder them for the rest of the leg.

Green Dragon led the fleet from the Doldrums, with PUMA and Ericsson 4 right on her tail. But the Dragon held her advantage through the scoring gate at Fernando de Noronha, followed by Ericsson 4, with PUMA just 17 minutes behind. The group was joined by Telefónica Black, who had staged a remarkable recovery from her western adventure at the Canary Islands, the clouds parting for them through the Doldrums, like the Red Sea before Moses. She was up into fourth by the scoring gate.

delta lloyd
delta lloyd
delta lloyd
delta lloyd
VOLVO
OCEAN
RACE
2008-2009

Slowly, the longer preparation time and bigger budgets of the two boats behind Green Dragon started to tell, and Ericsson 4 and PUMA broke through into the lead. The road south was a long one, as the fleet targeted a low-pressure front spinning up off the coast of Brazil. Everyone aboard each of the eight boats checked their area of responsibility as it became clearer just how tough the final days of sailing to Cape Town would be. After days of anxious anticipation, the front hit them on the morning of 28 October.

Aboard Ericsson 3, Martin Krite was twice swept from the bow. The first time the force of the water dumped him into the lifelines. The second time he was swept four or five metres along the deck in a blind chaos of foam until his legs were slammed into the daggerboard and his head hit the mast. He was helped back below. He stayed in his bunk for the rest of the watch, then resumed his duties on deck. But for the rest of the trip he couldn't look up without losing his balance. After a CT scan in Cape Town, the diagnosis was that the concussion and swelling had affected the balance nerve. But Krite dismissed any concern. "The Doldrums," he said. "That was the worst thing that has happened in my sailing career."

Green Dragon had dug themselves deep into the south, the closest to the centre of the low pressure. *"I think it may be time to open negotiations with Neal about taking the spinnaker down,"* wrote Ian Walker from the navigation station as the ante began to get upped. Neal McDonald was helming in the early hours of the morning, with the wind averaging around 30

left   Delta Lloyd blasts along with the wind coming from behind. The daggerboards are raised (either side of the mast) to lower the drag of the hull through the water when sailing in this mode, for they are not required to resist sideslip (or leeway) as they are when at other angles to the wind.

right Team Russia takes a
wave over the bow. Only the
windward daggerboard is
raised, because on this point
of sailing (a reach) the leeward
one is required to resist
sideslip (or leeway) through
the water.

knots from the north-west, when, with all the violence of a slow-motion car crash, the boat hit something and went from about 22 knots to less than seven.

McDonald was thrown forward with such force by the deceleration that the wheel rim snapped off the spoke. The boat staggered under the impact, but the sails filled again and she began to accelerate. Irish bowman Justin Slattery, an ABN AMRO ONE veteran, recovered his feet and grabbed the leeward wheel to keep control of the boat, until McDonald could free himself from the smashed and useless windward one. Unlike Stu Bannatyne aboard Ericsson 4, McDonald was tethered to the wheel pedestal to stop him being washed overboard, rather than to a jackstay that would allow him to cross the boat.

They had no idea how much damage had been done to the hull and fins, and could only wait anxiously for word from below as they tried to sort out the mess on deck. At least there was no one tumbling out of the hatch with lifejackets and emergency grab-bags. Finally, the stand-by watch appeared with the news that the boat didn't appear to be sinking – at least, not immediately. It was a full 10 minutes before they were happy that they weren't going to be sinking at all. And in the meantime, McDonald and the crew had resumed racing anyway. "You've fought for those metres," he said afterwards, "and you don't give them up easily."

Whatever they hit remained attached to the keel for a good few hours, vibrating horribly, before it was finally washed away. It left considerable damage to the hydrodynamically shaped carbon plates that smooth the water flow around the steel keel fin. The extra drag slowed them by about 10 percent for the rest of the leg – McDonald reckoned the damage created about 250 kilograms of extra resistance to the boat's forward motion. And with 1,500 miles to go, it put them out of the chase for a podium finish.

Telefónica Black was skippered by Fernando Echávarri, fresh from winning the Tornado Olympic gold medal in Beijing. The Black boat had been built late, joining her sister ship from the construction yard in New Zealand with just a couple of months left for two boat testing. Her navigator was the irrepressible Roger Nilson, a Swedish veteran whose first race was aboard Alaska Eagle in 1981–82, back in the days when there was a bottle or two of wine for dinner every night. Nilson admitted to an addictive personality in his 2007 autobiography, Towards the Eye of the Storm, and the Volvo Ocean Race was probably its least destructive outlet.

Nilson and Telefónica Black had the sort of roller-coaster ride up and down the first leg rankings that was almost, but not quite, a match for Nilson's previous buccaneering career. Starting with a drunken expedition down the west coast of Sweden in a half-decked five-metre boat at the age of 15, he had gone on to survive a stint as a naval reserve officer, hanging with the aristocratic sixties jetset in Mexico, a pirate attack in the Bahamas, a medical career, and open heart surgery six months before the race started.

Nilson knows his way around the planet, but there are plenty of unknowns and uncertainties in blue-water offshore racing, and at 17.40 GMT on 29 October, Telefónica Black found one of them. The leeward rudder sheered off just below the hull. The boat rolled on to its side, completely out of control, the sails flogging. Nilson was at his navigation station. He thought it was just another broach

top   Sunset at the helm for
Ericsson 3 – but no sundowners
for these guys: the crew will
race just as hard through the
night.

bottom   A thumbs up from
Telefónica Black as she pushes
a big chunk of ocean out of
the way.

and reached for his foul-weather gear. By the time he got on deck the headsail was gone; Argentinian crewman Maciel Cicchetti had cut it loose. But the sea had smashed away the bowsprit, and as the sail and all the gear came rushing aft, it had taken blocks off the deck. A deep wound had also been scored in the daggerboard, but if it hadn't been there, the rigging might have been damaged and brought the mast down instead. The crew set about clearing up the mess, and fixing the emergency rudder.

All this while, Ericsson 4 swept imperially eastwards, outrunning the opposition, the low-pressure front and the record. And then Stu Bannatyne heard and felt that bang. Something had hit the rudder. Immediately, he turned the boat away from the wind to wash off the speed, and David Endean went down below to check for damage.

Despite never quite finishing his apprenticeship at the legendary Cookson Boats, David Endean was boat captain for Ericsson 4. He was ultimately responsible for the yacht and all its systems. If there was a problem he would likely be the man to lead any repair team. He was a New Zealander, like Bannatyne, and, again like Bannatyne, he had won the race before – in Endean's case, the previous edition aboard ABN AMRO ONE. Still in his twenties, this was his third Volvo Ocean Race. There wasn't much he didn't know about these boats, even if learning it had got in the way of his trade certificate.

Endean climbed down the companionway and unhooked his safety tether, then grabbed a torch and crawled back down the boat. The rudders were in the furthest aft compartment, behind a watertight bulkhead door which they kept shut to reduce the noise.

He opened it with some trepidation, but when he shone the torch inside, everything looked normal: the steering gear and rudder stock were all fine. Whatever it was they had hit, it hadn't done any damage. He shut the door, crawled back on deck with the good news, and Bannatyne turned the burners back on.

It was about an hour and a half later that Endean finished his watch. He made a habit of going round the boat for a final check before he turned in for some sleep. But this time, when he opened the aft compartment door, water poured out. It was completely flooded, water swilling around the compartment. He yelled up on deck and immediately they slowed the boat down. At the very least it was the end of their challenge for the record, but was it more serious than that?

It was impossible to see from the outside. In that part of the boat there was only about a metre of headroom between the deck and the hull, narrowing further at the sides. The dark, cramped space was packed with bags of food, spares, clothing and electronics (including the satellite-communications terminal that transmitted their position and instrument data to the Race Office) – devices whose prospects of remaining functional seemed limited.

All the survival suits and spare ropes had broken free of the bags they had been stored in, and were now washing around the compartment, tying themselves into a knot of Gordian proportions. Floating on the surface was the grime that normally hid in the dark corners of their black carbon-fibre boat: hair, scraps of paper and a grey mulch, the origin of which no one liked to think too much about. And somewhere, buried in this mess, were the rudder posts – the likely source of the

leak. Endean climbed in and shut the watertight door behind him, to stem the flow of water into the rest of the boat.

With the deck hatch open instead, he started to pass everything up to clear the space. He wrestled the gear free of the tangle, even as he was washed around amongst it, gasping as the cold water flushed over him. Then the hatch fell shut. Plunged into semi-darkness, he was immediately dragged away from the exit by a surge of water. Survival suits and ropes grasped at his arms and legs, holding him down, and panic started to rise. He could see the hatch cover – it was opaque and the only source of light. Thrashing through the gear, he fought his way back to it and pounded on the plastic until it was opened. His subsequent outburst left his crewmates in no doubt about what he thought and the consequences should they let it happen again.

Endean eventually discovered that the rudder had been forced backwards in the boat by just seven millimetres, dragging the locking ring through the carbon fibre, and creating enough of a gap to let the ocean in. About £16,000 worth of electronics had blown up, leaking current into the hull, which, although they didn't know it at the time, was fast corroding the winch bases and rudder bearings. It took him the rest of his off-watch to repair the problem and clear up the mess, at the end of which he went back on deck.

Ericsson 4 had been slowed, but remained ahead of both the fleet and the cold front until it faded to the south. Ken Read and PUMA chased them home, finishing 12 hours behind. Everyone else was dropped by

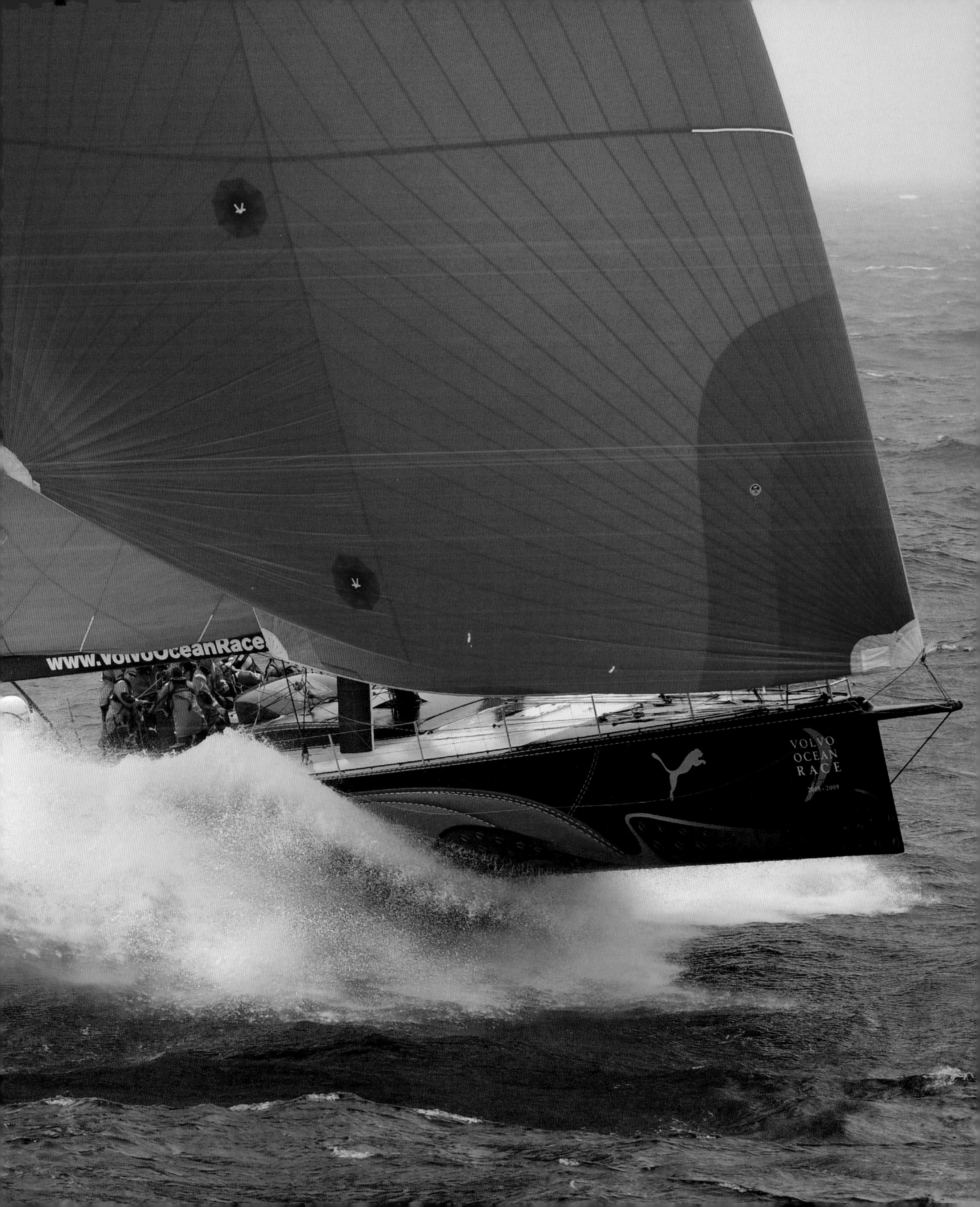

www.VolvoOceanRace
VOLVO
OCEAN
RACE

top   Breezy running conditions for PUMA. The sails have also been stacked at the back and on the windward side to help keep the boat level and the bow out of the water. Correct weight distribution for all the gear and people, both on deck and below, is crucial to optimum speed.

bottom   Sidney Gavignet steers PUMA downwind, with Rob Salthouse sitting behind him to trim sails. The use of a face mask, helmet, lifejacket and survival suit while on the wheel are common in these conditions, as there is no protection from wind and water for the helmsman.

overleaf   Ericsson 4 leads the spectator fleet into Cape Town – not long now before the crew will be reunited with family and friends, and welcome the opportunity to rest and recharge after more than three weeks of intense effort at sea.

the front and forced to detour to the south to find wind to take them to Cape Town. Ericsson 3 and the still-dazed Martin Krite did the best job of that, finally passing a wounded Green Dragon. Neal McDonald and his team-mates limped home fourth on the water, but were promoted to third after Ericsson 3 had a penalty applied for a keel infringement that was subsequently rectified in Cape Town.

Next were Jonathan Swain and Telefónica Blue, after a good recovery from the pit-stop at Gibraltar. The decision to change the tiller arms had been vindicated by the high loads that the rudder had had to withstand in the South Atlantic. But it could have been better; Swain explained afterwards that they were struggling to push the boat hard in the heavy running conditions of the final days, and passing opportunities had gone begging. They set to work on the problem in Cape Town.

Jeremy Elliott and Team Russia slid up to sixth in the home straight, gaining the benefit of holding their boat together. On arrival in Cape Town, Elliott would propose to his girlfriend, Jo (and be accepted). Delta Lloyd's broken strut meant they could only fly fractional spinnakers on starboard gybe, which left them in seventh place. Roger Nilson and Telefónica Black trailed home last, and when they pulled the boat out of the water in Cape Town there was evidence of impact damage to the bow and both rudders. They couldn't be sure this had caused the rudder failure, but it seemed very likely.

And eventually, the World Speed Sailing Record Council (WSSRC) pronounced on Ericsson 4's run, ratifying a new 24-hour monohull world record at a distance of 596.6 nautical miles, concluding at 18.55 on 29 October – after Endean had completed the repair to the back of the boat. The magical 600-mile barrier remained officially unbroken, but the rudder damage and subsequent instrument failure had come just when they were poised to break the 600 miles – both slowing them and forcing the Race Office to rely on back-up positioning systems to measure their progress. There was no question that 600 miles was now possible, but would they get another chance to put it in the record books?

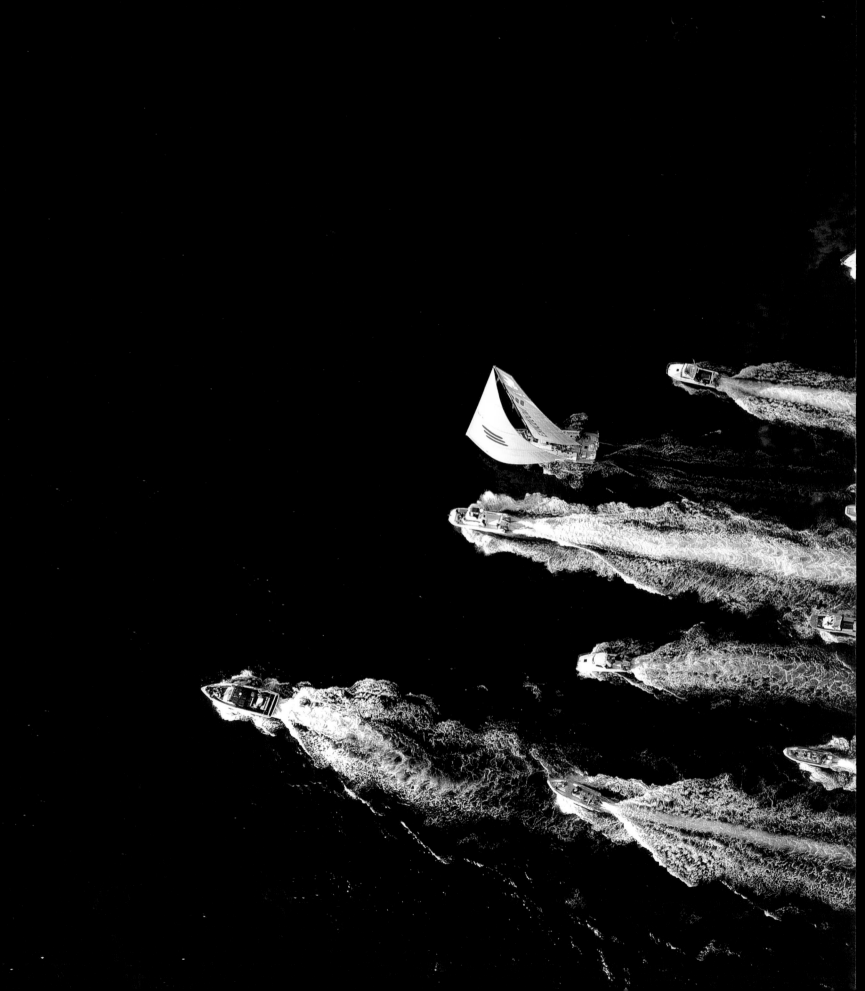

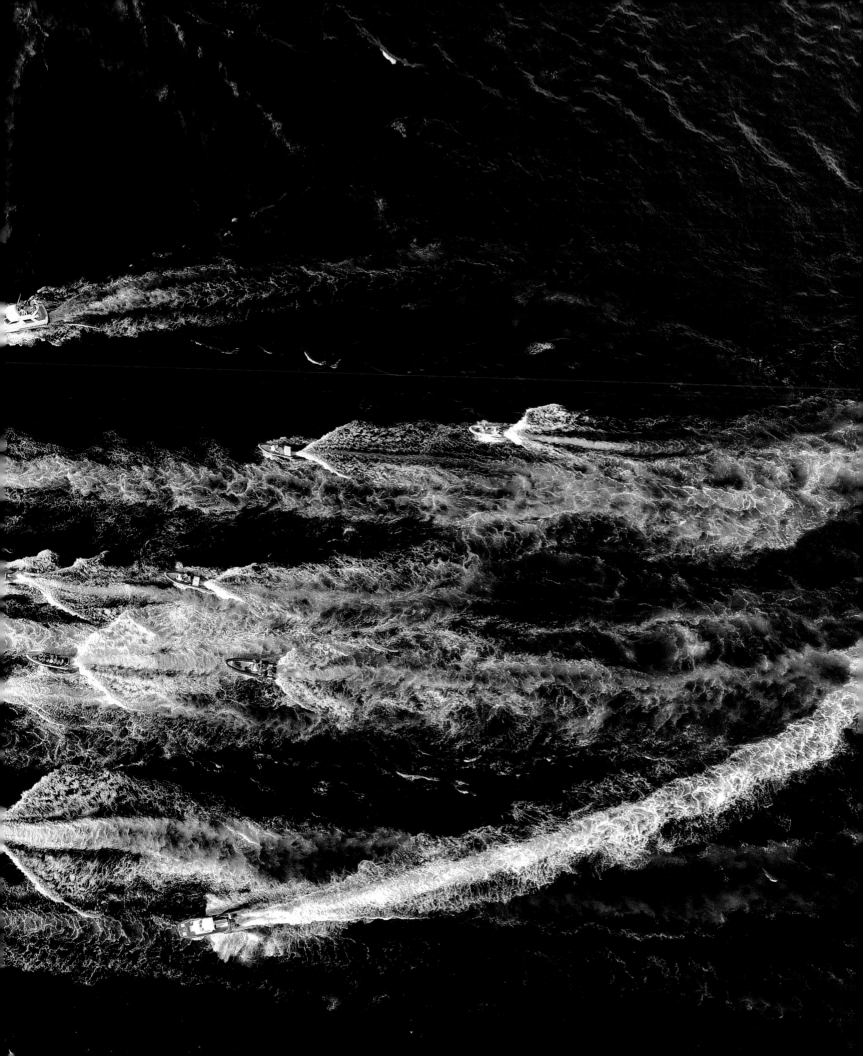

Running Repairs

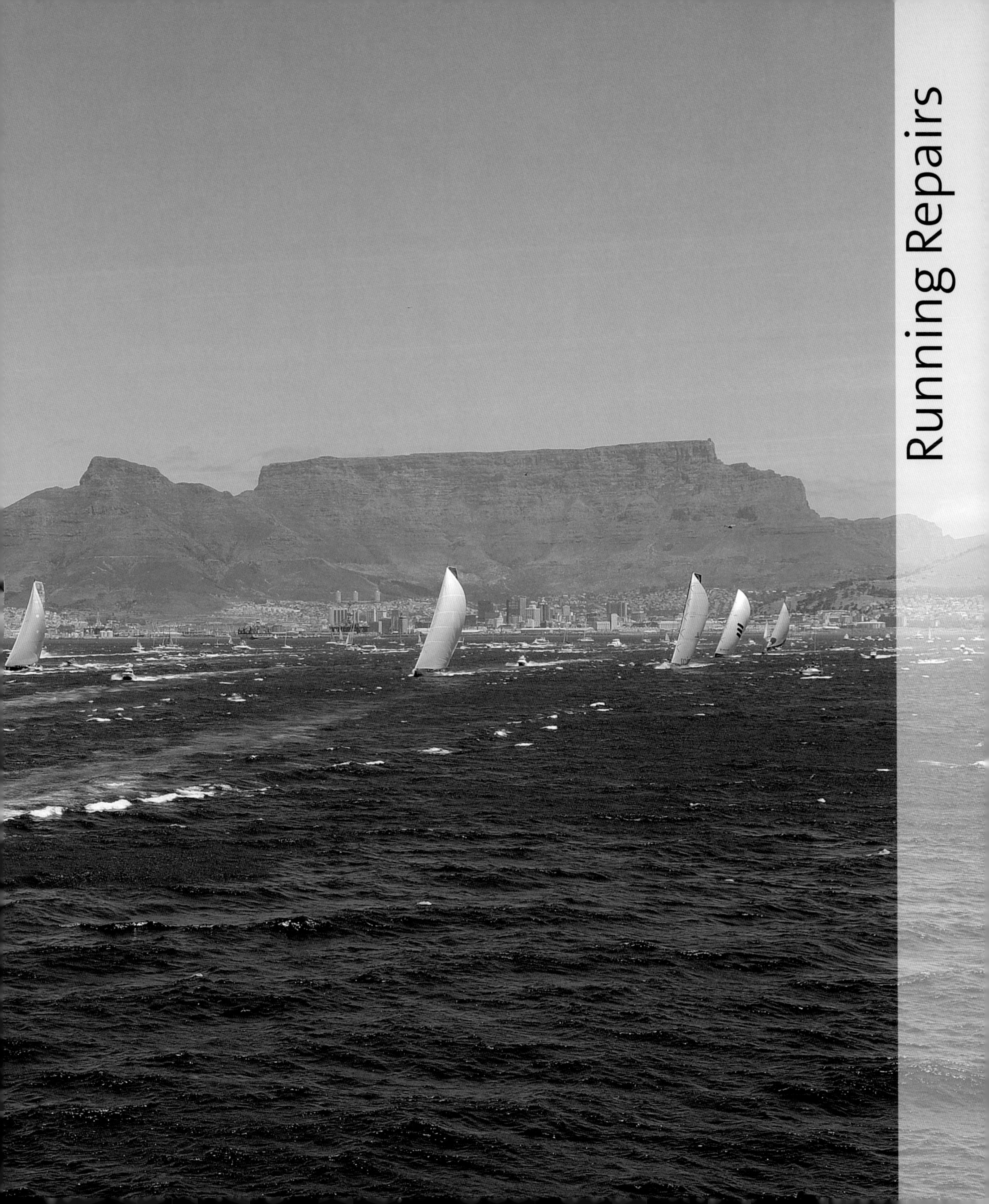

The familiar ring tone broke loudly into Neil Cox's sleep. It was still dark outside, and he was in a hotel room, that much he knew. PUMA's shore manager fumbled for the phone and saw the number – the +870 satellite code. It was the boat, pushing the leader hard, deep in the squalls and storms of the Southern Ocean. His stomach tightened. He liked to think they missed him, but they weren't ringing him at that hour to tell him so. He put the phone to his ear. It was the skipper, Ken Read. And they had a problem.

The second leg of the Volvo Ocean Race could not have begun any better for PUMA. Saturday 15 November, 2008, was a perfect Cape Town day, and PUMA came out of the starting blocks quicker than Usain Bolt. They blazed through a big and unruly spectator fleet to lead round the first two race buoys set off the city's waterfront, headed for a finish that was 4,450 nautical miles away across the Indian Ocean in Cochin, on the western coast of the subcontinent.

The quick start wasn't to last. The malign influence that Table Mountain could have on the winds of the bay had been absent for the finish of leg one. But now the mountain did its thing; the breeze died and PUMA ground to a halt. Like the Keystone Cops, the rest of the fleet had no choice but to follow them into the hole. Everyone held their breath.

But Table Mountain was just delivering a light cuff on the shoulder. PUMA lost the lead, but no one escaped south with more than a hair's breadth of advantage. And after a move offshore from the Cape Peninsula, Ken Read took PUMA back to the front, slugging it out with Torben Grael and Ericsson 4. On this occasion there

would be no anxious wait, the wind quickly veered as another low-pressure front hit them, the spinnakers went up and leg two started as leg one had finished – at a frantic pace. It was a drag race to the scoring gate, set at the line of longitude 58 deg E, and no one wanted to let Ericsson 4 sail away with it.

It wasn't long before the pace started to tell. Aboard Team Russia, Jeremy Elliott was asleep in his bunk, only to be woken by a sudden lurch and the violent pull of gravity as the world turned on its axis. The boat had slammed into the back of a wave, pushing green water all the way up to the mast. With the rudders out of the water and control gone, they capsized. Elliott was thrown against the carbon-fibre hull as it became the floor. The bunk collapsed on top of him, followed by anything that wasn't tied down. He struggled back to consciousness in a puddle of freezing bilge water, emerging disorientated from a heap of food bags, clothes, spare gear and people. It took a while to sort out the mess, but they were lucky – the only damage was a bent guardrail, and they had to cut some ropes to get the boat back upright. Fortunately, particularly for Elliott, the sails survived, and very soon they were on track once more.

Early on Tuesday morning, two and a half days after the start, the fleet were deep into the Southern Ocean. Ericsson 4 had a narrow lead to the scoring gate, with PUMA, Ericsson 3 and Green Dragon all close behind. Aboard PUMA, media crew member Rick Deppe had just put the kettle on. He braced himself against the unpredictable motion of the boat, distributing tea bags into cups.

chapter opener **PUMA leads the fleet against the glorious backdrop of Cape Town and Table Mountain.**

left **Leg two starts as it went on – fast and wet. The GPS and satellite communications antennas are all visible, mounted in the stern of the boat. They have to be completely waterproof for the electronics to survive months of this kind of treatment.**

left The bowman on Ericsson 4 is raised aloft to work on one of the big furling headsails. Notice the protective cables around the front of the white radar dome, mounted on the mast a few metres off the deck. This is to stop the sail-handling ropes from getting tangled around it – a problem for Ericsson 3 at the start in Cape Town.

right The bowman's job is the most physically demanding on the boat. Up at the sharp end, they are wrestling with heavy, unwieldy sails on an often violently mobile platform.

top Rick Tomlinson (still photography, left) and Matt Connor (video, right) cover the Cape Town start from a helicopter. Wherever possible these two cameramen were airborne for the action, as it gave a completely different perspective to that provided by the onboard media crew.

bottom PUMA's media crew Rick Deppe films the action. Deppe relied on a large amount of what would normally be considered fragile electronic equipment, much of which had to be protected from sea water and vibration. Deppe's full equipment list was as follows: Sony HVR-A1U and HDR-HC9 video cameras, the latter with highly modified sport housing; Nikon D90 and D80 cameras with a Pclix intervalometer; Canon G9 camera; Sony HXR-MC1 POV camera; Audio-Technica wireless microphones; Marantz digital audio recorder.

A former professional sailor, his path into the sport had been remarkably similar to Jonathan Swain's. Deppe had also headed for America and ended up in Annapolis. And there, again like Swain, he had met both his future wife, Anastasia, and been hired for the Chessie Racing Whitbread campaign as bowman. He then volunteered to work as the onboard cameraman. A decade ago the role used to be filled by a regular crewman, and fitted in around all the other demands. By the time the race was finished, Deppe knew that film was his new passion. So he followed the same principle that he had used with sailing: go to the work.

He flew to LA and through a sailing contact got a job on a reality television show called Drive Shaft. It led to the Discovery Channel, where he worked as an editor, in-house cameraman and studio manager, until one day, when the producers of Drive Shaft called and asked if he'd like to work as a cameraman on a new show: Deadliest Catch. The Emmy Award–nominated hit confirmed his career transition, just as he started to miss sailing. So when Ken Read got in touch to ask if he was interested in the role of media crew aboard PUMA, it seemed like the perfect opportunity to combine both.

It wasn't a particularly big lurch as they took off from the back of a wave, but Deppe was as attuned as any other crew member to the meaning of the particularly loud crack that came from the forward compartment when they landed. He knew that somewhere, carbon fibre had broken. He raised the alarm and soon they were crawling around the front of the boat with torches, looking for damage. It didn't take long to find: a crack in a structural I-beam, placed longitudinally to stiffen the big open areas of carbon-

fibre panel from which the boat was constructed. The beam was secondary structure, so they weren't sinking. As the crew took a more detailed look, Rick Deppe took photos. His priorities were different from everyone else's – as the media crew member, he was there to record events, not participate.

There is a certain tension in the role of the media crew member, placed there by the Race Office to ensure a steady stream of images and stories from each boat. Deppe was a passenger; forbidden by the rules from contributing to the sailing, he remained a spectator, watching and filming as his crewmates struggled with each new challenge. So he was wary at first, conscious of how disappointed they would be at this turn of events. He filmed tactfully, picking his moments to ask questions on camera. But nevertheless, when Ken Read phoned Neil Cox that Tuesday morning, Rick Deppe's primary concern was his camera angle, the lighting and the sound quality.

The same could not be said for Neil Cox. PUMA's shore manager had lived and breathed the boat since her conception, and he was struggling to take in Ken Read's description of the damage as he woke up. But the adrenaline was pumping, and moments later he was asking questions, going down a prepared process to establish exactly what the problem was and how they might fix it. Cox asked Rick Deppe to take detailed pictures of the damage, and send them back by email as fast as he could. And as soon as he hung up, Cox was dialling again, gathering the team, putting the plan into action.

For Neil Cox – shore manager for the all-conquering ABN AMRO ONE in the 2005–06 Volvo Ocean Race – this was familiar territory. But Cox didn't

left Ducking an incoming wave aboard Ericsson 3. However good your foul-weather gear, it's still better not to take a wave in the face if you can avoid it!

grow up in a family steeped in sailing and its eccentric traditions. He was brought up in a Sydney suburb called Turramurra, meaning 'hill with a view', although home was actually at the bottom of a valley. Five miles distant, the Ku-Ring-Gai Chase National Park bordered a secluded estuary. It had all Sydney Harbour's natural beauty, but a fraction of its development. And it had Bobbin Head, with its boatyards and all the beguiling life that goes on within and around them. Not much interested in school, Neil Cox wanted to build things, and the waterfront seemed a desirable place to work. At 15, he started a four-year apprenticeship with a timber boatbuilder: Halvorsen Boats.

It didn't take long to get interested in sailing, or to figure out that he was never going to get rich building wooden boats, so he applied for a job as a boatbuilder with the OneAustralia America's Cup team in 1995. He was 23, and since then home has been whatever hotel or apartment the project has taken him to. But however much experience you've got, the middle-of-the-night phone call from a worried skipper is never pleasant. So Cox started to pull together all the resources from around the world: the team's general manager, Kimo Worthington in the USA; PUMA's designers, Marcelino Botín and Shaun Carkeek in Santander, northern Spain; and the structural engineers, Julien Sellier in England and Fredrick Louaran in France.

At about the same time aboard Green Dragon, the engineer Tom Braidwood was recovering from a torrid 24 hours. First, they had discovered a leak in the daggerboard case on the port side, where a carbon-fibre seam had separated. Watch captain Damian Foxall did

his best impression of the little Dutch boy at the dyke, keeping his finger pressed against the failed seam to stop the water coming in, while Braidwood climbed into the stern compartment to find the toolkit and spares.

Neal McDonald was on the wheel (minus wedding ring) and as usual, had the boat flat out, sailing right on the edge of control, when there was a huge bang just feet from Braidwood's head. The steering gear had failed. The boat instantly rolled into a carbon copy of the Team Russia capsize – but quick thinking saved them. This time it was the Australian trimmer, Anthony Merrington, who grabbed the still-functioning leeward wheel. He got the boat turning back the right way before the mast could hit the water.

Once disentangled from the jumble of gear in the stern compartment, Braidwood assessed the two lots of damage and decided to stem the leak first. Three bolts and a lot of sealant later, the flow had been stopped. Next was the steering gear – a pulley had separated from the hull. Its positioning was critical for the smooth functioning of the steering, but it could no longer be fastened to the same spot. Nor could it be screwed down anywhere else, without the necessary localised strengthening for the fastenings. They improvised by drilling a hole in the side of the hull and gluing a reinforcing plate to the outside, and then hanging the pulley from a strop passed through the hole. It worked perfectly.

The engineers aboard the Volvo Open 70s have many and various qualifications. Tom Braidwood had started his working life as a diesel maintenance fitter on the Australian railways. His headmaster had 'suggested' he leave school at the earliest opportunity, and Braidwood was persuaded to try the entrance exam for

top Green Dragon's boom breaks during a 50-knot squall in the Southern Ocean. The immediate challenge is to stop it doing any further damage to the boat, sails or rig.

bottom The situation is now under control. With the boom detached from the sail and safely on the deck, the crew can now start to strip it off the mast and get it down below, before making a decision on whether or not to try to repair it.

the apprenticeship by a friend. As is often the way with these things, Braidwood passed, while his mate didn't. He lasted a year with the railways after completing his apprenticeship, before heading for Sydney and a job with a rigging company.

Braidwood's family had a sailing history; his father had raced the Sydney to Hobart with Rupert Murdoch back in the 1960s, and introduced Tom to the sailing scene on Lake Macquarie. The link was broken for a while after his parents divorced, but others at the sailing club helped to direct some of Tom's anger into going sailing despite his father, to better his father's achievements. And if there's one thing about Tom Braidwood, it's his unstoppable determination.

He tried out for and got a place as a bowman and rigger with the poor relation of the two Australian teams challenging for the 1995 America's Cup. All he knew was that he knew next to nothing, but he learned fast, and he met people; he shared a room with Neal McDonald. So when the Whitbread Race arrived in Fremantle, Western Australia, in 1997, he flew himself across the country, found McDonald and offered his services – for free. Before McDonald left, Braidwood had been hired for the rest of the race to help with the rigging and mast maintenance.

By the time the first Volvo Ocean Race came round in 2001, Tom Braidwood's attitude and abilities had got him a place on the crew of the yacht SEB. And the sailing had brought him close to his father again. Enormously proud of Tom's achievements, his father planned to visit the stopover ports and follow the adventure around the world. Sadly, he didn't live to see the race start.

Tom Braidwood can fix pretty much anything on a Volvo Open 70, but he's still a sailor, and he was happy to get up on deck and do some sailing on that Tuesday morning, after the long stint of repairs. The squall was nothing unusual for the Southern Ocean, 50 knots coming in under a cloud line. They had the headsail furled in plenty of time, and were running before the storm with just the mainsail up – completely under control. Then the boom broke. It came as a complete surprise; Braidwood said afterwards they had no idea why it happened, that this was the first such breakage in three races. But the immediate problem was to get the boom off the sail, before the shattered carbon fibre did more damage. And then they had to work out how they were going to get to India.

In the end, it was Rick Deppe's photos of PUMA's broken longitudinal I-beam that put Neil Cox's mind at ease, for it immediately showed him that the problem was repairable at sea. Once they had a plan, it took just three hours to strengthen the structure. And six hours after that, the boat was topping 40 knots again. But Cox went on with his checks – buckling tests, finite element analysis (FEA) calculations, modelling the hull's structural integrity without the longitudinal I-beam there at all – pushing the engineers until they were absolutely sure that the boat was safe. And 19 hours after the phone had first rung, Neil Cox climbed, exhausted, back into bed. It was done. He was happy, the problem was resolved and the boat was sound.

Three hours later, the phone rang again. Mind blurry with fatigue, Cox scrabbled for his mobile. Later, Ken Read reported the second failure in an email: *"Three of us were having breakfast at the time and there was a bit of a stare into each other's eyes* [when they *right* The bowman is caught in silhouette behind PUMA's headsail, a sail largely constructed from Kevlar fibre laminated between clear plastic film, on which the graphics are printed. The rules insisted that the Volvo Open 70s had to carry storm sails, to which the crew could add a mainsail, up to four headsails and up to five spinnakers, of which three could be hoisted all the way to the top of the mast.

top A mug of Twinings finest Earl Grey tea and a snack meant a brief moment of normality after enduring the Southern Ocean. Notice how a safety hitch has been tied in the end of the rope coming off the winch drum. Ropes have been known to slip out of the self-tailing device on the top of the winch.

bottom Once the fleet turned north out of the Southern Ocean, they had to negotiate an area of high pressure and light winds, which provided the opportunity to dry everything out. But the transition from foul-weather gear to shorts and T-shirts was short-lived.

heard the crack].
'That didn't sound good,' said Justin Ferris.
'Nope,' I said.
Chris Nicholson added, 'Maybe it was just an unloaded sheet snapping up on deck?'
Justin looked down and said, 'Or maybe it was this large crack splitting the main longitudinal frame?'
The master of understatement, old Justin."

And now Neil Cox was wide awake and starting over, with a new and bigger problem. The PUMA team had reduced their spares to 40 per cent of normal, in expectation of a light-wind leg, and now they were short of materials. Afterwards he described it as like a poor man's version of the Apollo 13 mission: "With just these materials, we have to fix that, OK … so, how do we do it?" But Cox and his team of designers and engineers came up with a solution; sketches and instructions were emailed to the boat, and the tools came out and the work began again. Carbon dust started to fill the hull, working its way into clothes, sleeping bags and hair.

Meanwhile, Ken Read and his navigator, Andrew Cape, worked on a strategy to minimise their losses while the repairs were done. Rick Deppe kept filming and editing, pleased with the relaxed and open manner in which the crew had handled his questions. And Neil Cox kept planning, phoning and calculating. However good the repair they did now, he still had to find a way to fix the boat properly in India. It would be three and a half days before he found time to leave his hotel room, and eat something other than room service.

The team aboard Green Dragon had worked out a way to control the mainsail without their broken boom, which was now safely down below. Still third in the race to the scoring gate, skipper Ian Walker decided to postpone any attempt at repair, so that they could focus on sailing the boat to get maximum points at the gate. But that didn't stop Tom Braidwood from making plans – to start with, could they get the boom they had brought down the hatch in two pieces, back up it in one?

The combination of the damage to Green Dragon and PUMA had left the two Ericsson boats with a clear run at the scoring gate. Despite the handicap, Green Dragon held on to third, chased all the way by a charging Team Russia, but it was Ericsson 4 that led her sister ship across the line for a one-two and maximum points. The gap between the pair was just over three hours – a marked improvement on their leg one performance for Martin Krite and the team on Ericsson 3, who had reaped the benefits of a long and thorough debrief in Cape Town. Eight of the crew hadn't been in the Southern Ocean before, and they had made a big effort to learn from leg one, when Krite had taken such a battering. They sorted out the lines of communication – easily confused by the multiplicity of languages amongst the international crew – partly by the basic step of ensuring that when everyone was required on deck in a hurry, they took the time to get to their normal positions.

And, Krite admitted afterwards, they kept it simple – no more complex sail changes more appropriate to his background in the America's Cup. Martin Krite came into professional sailing through the Lerums Seglargymnasium, one of three specialist sailing high schools in Sweden. Each of them teaches promising students a conventional school curriculum, along with a great deal of the theory and practice that goes into

making a top professional sailor. It's a system that is used in other sports in the country, including ice hockey, soccer and snowboarding. His rise was swift, particularly once he specialised in keel boats and match racing. In 2003, at the age of 22, Krite sailed the whole of the Louis Vuitton Cup series with Victory Challenge. It was after returning to the team in preparation for the 2007 event that he quit sailing to study theology. And now he was being forced to unlearn, or at least adapt, many of the techniques learned in those America's Cup years.

Once through the scoring gate, the fleet turned north for India, leaving the Southern Ocean behind them. And it was David Endean who had the last word on racing in this part of the world, with an email from Ericsson 4: *"I prefer this gybe on our boat. The toilet is much easier to use when it is on the leeward side. The galley is much harder to use, but you don't have your pants down in the galley, so you can deal with it."*

The next challenge was a ridge of high pressure barring the road northwards. The fleet skirted round it, with the two Ericsson boats maintaining their advantage at the front. One side-effect was a day of lighter winds, which provided a welcome opportunity to dry out boats, clothes and people. But soon they reached the southeast trade winds, the speeds built and spray was again hurled constantly across the deck. Read and Cape's strategy had taken PUMA north a little earlier than the others, to keep them in touch with the leaders, and the price had been seventh place at the scoring gate. Now with the boat repaired, confidence was returning and they were racing at full speed.

Green Dragon's plans to fly a spare boom to the American base on the island of Diego Garcia came to nothing, after the authorities refused permission for the boat to land to collect it. But Ian Walker continued to postpone the repair, which he felt would be a distraction, as the team worked out even better ways to trim the mainsail without it. Still, Tom Braidwood developed his plans, which involved a piece of alloy steering bar, a lot of spare sail battens, a sheet of Kevlar and carbon weave, fastenings, resin and a great deal of glue.

Aboard Telefónica Blue, South African watch captain Jonathan Swain and his team-mates were relieved to be headed north. They had been under enormous pressure through the Southern Ocean, missing helmsman Laurent Pages, whose shoulder was badly damaged when a wave threw him into the steering pedestal guard. Many of the crew went down with a vomiting bug – possibly due to infected water that they took on in Cape Town, or something that was not filtered out by the watermaker. So when two sails in succession ripped and needed repair they were desperately short-handed on deck, and forced to add two hours to each watch.

Despite this they held on to fifth place at the scoring gate, just eight hours behind Ericsson 4. Just like Ericsson 3, the work they did in Cape Town had paid dividends. They had changed the watch pairings to better utilise each individual's strengths. They had modified some of the sails, and at the suggestion of the designers – Farr Yacht Design – they had changed the way they sailed the boat. It all worked, and now, with the sickness cleared up, the sails repaired and the trade-wind reaching conditions to the boat's liking, this was their time to shine. They charged through the fleet under a bright blue sky, with 15 knots of boat speed in 18 knots of

left **A cloud belt looms ahead of Ericsson 3. The system varied on different boats, but usually the navigator would use the radar to assess what impact the cloud might have on the wind, and then discuss the strategy with the watch captain.**

top   Working on the mainsail on Team Russia; notice the safety line attached to the bowman's harness and running back down to the deck. This is in case he falls off the back of the mainsail and swings uncontrollably to leeward – the safety line can be used to pull him back into the boat. Some of the gear, like the bowman's harness and karabiners, has been derived from climbing equipment.

bottom   Trade-wind sailing on Telefónica Blue. Although the water and the air are warm, the sailing can still be hard, with constant spray driving across the deck.

wind. It was a perfect day, Swain reflected, as he went below to make a cup of tea. It couldn't last. And it didn't. Just as he poured the water into the mugs, there was a stomach-churning crash as the daggerboard shattered.

Suspended in the water from a rope, it took 40 minutes for bowman Pepe Ribes to cut the damaged section from below the hull, and then for the rest of the crew to pull the broken board out from above. Initially, they didn't lose too many miles, but the deficits kept coming. The wind was slowly rotating to blow from north of east, and they needed the daggerboard's resistance to leeway; without it, they were getting helplessly pushed to the west, and separated from the leading group of the two Ericsson boats, PUMA and Green Dragon.

It was a critical moment; they were about to recross the Doldrums, this time from south to north. If anyone needed reminding how important it was to enter in the right place, they only needed to think back to Green Dragon's winning move in the Atlantic. The clouds gathered over the fleet, the wind faded and, to the frustration of her crew, Telefónica Blue slid inexorably westwards. Meanwhile, Jeremy Elliott and his colleagues aboard Team Russia had made a big move to the east, where the weather forecasts indicated a much narrower and faster Doldrums transit. Then, in the space of 24 hours, it all changed.

Ericsson 4 disappeared into a rain cloud just a few miles from Ericsson 3, PUMA and Green Dragon – and emerged 30 miles in front and almost free of the Doldrums. The latter three remained stuck, while Delta Lloyd closed a 35-mile deficit to sail up to them from behind. Out to the east, Team Russia shuddered to a halt

as they found themselves enveloped in a huge windless hole. But to the west, the clouds cleared, the breeze came in and Telefónica Blue took off in pursuit of the fast-escaping Ericsson 4. The forecasts were wrong, and these two boats extended leads in excess of 100 miles, comfortably holding first and second to the finish.

It was a dominant performance from the team on Ericsson 4, who had taken maximum points from the leg and opened their overall lead to seven points from Telefónica Blue. Behind them, Ericsson 3 was doing a much improved job in their second Doldrums transit – it was no less a nightmare, according to Martin Krite, but they knew the frustrations, and how to deal with them. They worked hard at staying with the fleet and winning the small battles, rather than relying on a grand strategy. And they did it well, maintaining a narrow advantage to finish third.

Green Dragon, PUMA and Delta Lloyd emerged from the Doldrums together in a grim, tight battle to the finish line. They didn't give much thought to Telefónica Black, who had also snapped a daggerboard and sagged to the west in the wake of her sister ship – an event that for many spectators seemed to discount collisions as probable causes. But now they were also gaining from their western positioning, and fast closing on the preoccupied group in front of them.

It was their Swedish navigator, adventurer Roger Nilson, who provided the winning master stroke, when on the final morning he directed Telefónica Black into the coast. And as the land heated under the scorching Indian sun, the hotter, lighter air started to rise and pull in cooler air from the sea to replace it. Telefónica Black picked up this thermally generated 'sea breeze' first,

top   The new route took the Volvo Ocean Race to new audiences. Here, Telefónica Blue's skipper Bouwe Bekking gets a grilling from the Indian media after their arrival into Cochin.

bottom   India was a very different destination from the ones the crews were used to from previous editions of the race, a message constantly reinforced during the stopover!

sailing round the others into fourth place. PUMA chased Telefónica Black home to get fifth, and Delta Lloyd beat Green Dragon for sixth place. The Dragon's skipper, Ian Walker, had remained resolute in his refusal to let Tom Braidwood have a go at repairing their boom all the way to the finish line. And, Braidwood admitted afterwards, it was the right decision – it would have been more distraction than benefit.

As soon as the boats touched the dock in Cochin, Neil Cox had his team working hard on PUMA. New, prefabricated sections had been built in the USA, then shipped to India as excess luggage in a surfboard bag – unconventional, but effective. The shore team worked 18-hour days in shifts to fit them, and the boat went back into the water on time.

They were a full two days into the repair when Jeremy Elliot and Team Russia finally arrived in Cochin. Their eastern strategy had unravelled badly, and there was only bitter disappointment and a very slow sail home in last place. Their consolation was one of the most spectacular welcomes ever seen for a Volvo Open 70: tens of thousands of people screamed and cheered as they pulled up to the dock during the official opening night of the Race Village. The crew made their way to the stage with spectators 50 deep behind the barriers and struggling to get close enough to shake hands and get autographs. It was a surreal and overwhelming experience for 11 men who had spent almost three weeks in the isolation of the Indian Ocean.

Real Life

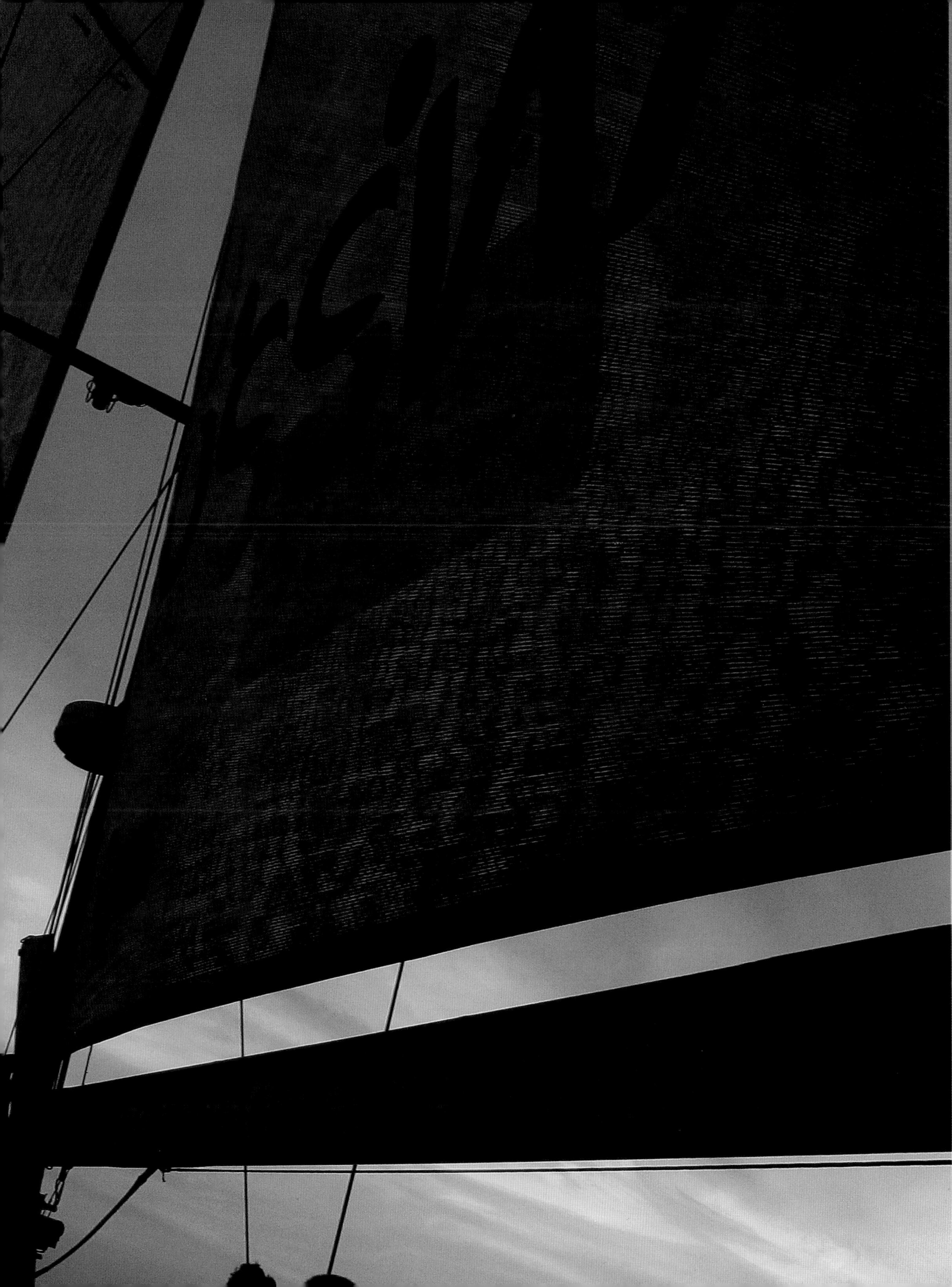

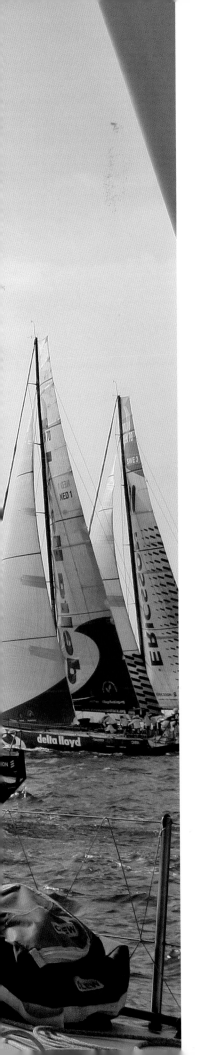

The route for leg three took the fleet 1,950 nautical miles, from Cochin east across the Indian Ocean to the northern end of the Malacca Strait, then south to Singapore. After three months of intense racing, with little in the way of respite at the short stopovers, everyone involved could be forgiven for starting to feel a little detached from life back home – wherever that might be.

The illusory bubble that the race forms around the unwary had been easy to maintain in the days when the fleet crossed the Southern Ocean to Cape Horn, with nothing but albatrosses and whales for company. But the new route took them north, through the busy waters of southern Asia – and 'real life' was about to intrude, though not in quite the way that everyone had worried about.

Back in Cape Town there had been warnings of piracy, terrorism and human traffickers when the Race Office organised a security briefing by Dryad Maritime Intelligence Service, focusing on the three legs that would take the race west to east across the bottom of Asia. For Roger Nilson, the navigator aboard Telefónica Black, these warnings had been particularly uncomfortable. Nilson had already been the target of an attack while transiting the Bahamas Channel aboard a sailing boat in 1981, just before the start of his Whitbread career on Alaska Eagle. They had fended off the pirates for long enough for a tanker to come to their aid, but it was an experience he was anxious not to repeat.

As if that wasn't unsettling enough, Nilson had also had a deeply distressing experience during the stopover in Cochin. Situated in the state of Uttar Pradesh, the Hindu temple at Radha-Kund is considered by Vaishnava Hindus as the holiest of all places. While

visiting a Swedish friend staying at a nearby ashram, they joined a huge crowd for a ceremony on the flat roof of the temple. Nilson left to find a toilet and phone his wife. Twenty minutes later, and just 30 seconds after his friend had crossed to the stairs to look for him, the roof collapsed. The result was tragic and bloody, and with no officials or police, never mind ambulances or medical supplies, Nilson found there was almost nothing he could do to help the injured and dying. He returned to the Race Village shaken and horrified by the experience.

The fleet started leg three on 13 December, leaving behind a Race Village packed with well-wishers. The course took them south, straight down the coast in conditions as light and difficult as those that had characterised the finish of leg two. After a slow start, Green Dragon was first to make an impact. She separated from the fleet, going inshore to the beach and picking up a light breeze off the land. She jumped from last to first while the others were becalmed. But everyone got a blast of the northeasterly monsoon wind – filtering between Sri Lanka and the southern tip of India – and Telefónica Blue soon chased her down.

In order to keep the fleet away from the coast of troubled Sri Lanka, two 'pirate waypoints' had been set, and proved to be quite a hurdle as the wind died again, leaving the boats struggling against a strong current to obey the rule. It was not an issue to be taken lightly, and Ericsson 3 was subsequently docked one point by the International Jury for straying into the exclusion zone for less than four minutes.

It was their sister ship, Ericsson 4, that played the light, shifting wind and adverse current best, to round

chapter opener **Perfect conditions; enjoy them while you can …**

left **The bowman aboard Green Dragon indicates with a hand signal that there are three boat lengths to the start line in Cochin, as the fleet accelerates ahead of the gun. Hand signals are the most reliable form of communication in the often loud and frenetic moments before the** start, but the meaning can vary between bowmen – it's always good for them to go through it with the helmsman before they get into the start sequence!

left Two strategies to deal with the problem of being constantly soaked by sea-water spray on the bow of Team Russia: wear as little as possible, or wear full foul-weather clothing. The first means dealing with the saltwater as it dries on your skin, the second means dealing with the salt sweat as it dries on your skin.

right Justin Slattery, bowman on Green Dragon, hangs over the side of the hull to check that the foils (keel fin, daggerboards and rudders) are all clear of weed or other rubbish that might become attached and slow the boat down. The crew can usually feel when something is slowing the boat, but regular checks help with peace of mind.

right   Watch captain Sidney Gavignet is hoisted up the mast of PUMA to get a better vantage point. While he can see what might otherwise be over the horizon, the most useful benefit is that in these light winds, Gavignet can see the patterns of ripples on the water, and glean useful information about the breeze to relay to the crew on deck.

the pirate waypoint in the lead. Telefónica Blue and PUMA were chasing them hard, but quickly found that they were not yet out of the grip of the current. One of the fleet's slowest days followed, with no one managing much more than 120 miles in 24 hours. Telefónica Blue discovered the solution first: there was less current to the south, and Jonathan Swain and his team slipped back into the lead. But then they allowed a significant separation to open to the rest of the fleet, who took the opportunity of a shifting wind to edge back north, towards the stronger breeze of the northeast monsoon. Telefónica Blue soon found herself alone in the south, with Bekking desperate for another wind shift to get across to where Ericsson 4 led the northern pack.

Trailing in the wake of that pack on the early evening of 18 December was Delta Lloyd. Gerd-Jan Poortman had just taken five minutes for a toilet break – right at the moment when there came the tearing crash of highly loaded, failing carbon fibre. Caught with his trousers down, both literally and metaphorically, he rushed up on deck expecting to see the mast in pieces. But there was nothing wrong on deck; the noise had come from down below. Grabbing a torch, he looked in all the obvious places – chainplates, bulkheads – while others removed the top from the keel wet-box. And there was the problem: one of the powerful hydraulic rams that cant the keel from one side to the other had torn loose from its carbon-fibre base. Immediately, a well-rehearsed routine started: safety gear from the lockers, bilge pumps prepared, headsail down on deck, and a phone call to the Race Office to advise them of the situation.

left   Ericsson 4 sails with the
wind from a line of dark cloud.
The crews had to be
constantly attentive to what
was going on in the skies
above them, as it was often
the best clue to an imminent
change in the conditions.

The keel was centralised using the other, still-functioning ram, while the damage was made safe: the broken ram was lashed so it couldn't punch a hole in the hull. That done, they called the designer, Juan Kouyoumdjian (also responsible for the two Ericsson boats), for advice. By the next morning, with the help of his structural-engineering team, they had calculated some answers: Delta Lloyd could safely sail at up to 20 degrees of heel, using the keel canted on the one ram, and didn't need to be concerned about pounding into waves. They began to nurse the boat home, eventually finishing safely in Singapore, and gathering the points for last place. The effort won them the Wallenius Wilhelmsen Logistics Seamanship Award for the second time in three legs; it was picked up by Edwin O'Connor, the boat captain.

Limping into port for two out of three finishes was, for Gerd-Jan Poortman, a curious reversal of circumstance from the previous race. Born in 's-Hertogenbosch in the south of the Netherlands, like so many others his sailing career had begun in dinghies (the Optimist), then switched to yachts when the cost had made it impossible to continue competing at the top level. He had been a contemporary of Jeremy Elliott's while at college in Southampton, and his first breakthrough had been a job as bowman on a top Dutch yacht, sailed by Andrew Cape (PUMA's navigator), amongst other luminaries.

The second breakthrough had come when he had applied, via the ABN AMRO team's website, for the open selection system for their under-30 crew. Poortman had been one of eight chosen from more than 1,800 applications. He was bowman on ABN AMRO TWO,

racing the sister ship to winner ABN AMRO ONE, the yacht that had in turn become Delta Lloyd. And TWO had sailed around the world largely unhindered by mechanical or structural problems, while all around them the rest of the fleet had fallen apart – often arriving at finish ports on container ships, or most memorably on the back of a truck. That said, the 2005–06 race was not without incident for Poortman – he'd chipped a vertebra and dislocated his coccyx after being washed into a daggerboard by a wave, forcing him to miss four legs, including the one that rounded the legendary Cape Horn.

And then there was the tragic death of Hans Horrevoets, lost overboard from TWO in the North Atlantic. The team recovered their crewmate, but couldn't revive him. The loss of a close friend badly affected Poortman. He gave up the professional sailing circuit, bought a house and settled down with his girlfriend, Evelien, in Utrecht. But, as time passed, he realised that he wasn't done with the Volvo Ocean Race. And so, when Delta Lloyd's Ger O'Rourke phoned him just a few days before the start in Alicante, and his employer, North Sails, then agreed to give him the time off as a sabbatical, Poortman's answer had been yes.

While Poortman and his team-mates struggled, the fleet was closing on the scoring gate: a line of longitude running north from the Indonesian island of Pulau We, at the northern end of the Malacca Strait. Telefónica Blue didn't get the shift in wind direction that she needed to rescue her from the southern position, and Ericsson 4 drove right past to pick up maximum points. It seemed that normal service had been resumed. But

right   Simon Fisher (left),
Pablo Arrate (right) and Daryl
Wislang (background) haul a
sail out of the main hatch of
Telefónica Blue. Notice the
black bar with green tape at
the base of the hatch; this is a
roller on bearings to make it
easier to slide the sails out.
There's also plenty of storage
for stuff that might need to be
grabbed quickly from around
the edges of the hatches.

no one had any illusions about the trip down the strait
to Singapore. From aboard Ericsson 4, watch captain Stu
Bannatyne wrote: *"It looks like the traditionally light air
passage ahead will give us plenty of headaches. We will
be preparing our anchor, and getting ourselves in the
mindset for some very busy wind seeking."*

It was more prophetic than he could have
imagined. At first, everything went smoothly for
Ericsson 4. Sticking to the middle of the channel, they
dodged the troublesome clouds that dogged Telefónica
Blue on the Indonesian coast. Aboard the Blue boat,
Jonathan Swain, Bouwe Bekking and company were
caught by PUMA and Ericsson 3, and in the brawl, gains
and losses were measured in metres, not miles, as they
clawed their way across the strait towards the Malaysian
beaches. Ericsson 4 maintained their middle-of-the-
straits strategy – and their 30-mile lead.

But when the sun rose on the penultimate
morning, the northeasterly monsoon wind that had
funnelled through the Thai and Malaysian valleys
expired. There was nothing to replace it except a weak
sea breeze on the beach, where PUMA, Telefónica Blue
and Ericsson 3 had positioned themselves. Suddenly, for
the first time in the race, the polished Ericsson 4
machine was in trouble – becalmed in the channel,
while three boats closed down their lead. Realising their
mistake, the team on Ericsson 4 reacted quickly, and
used what wind they had to get inshore, just catching
the tail end of the group.

As the sun set, it was clear to Jonathan Swain on
Telefónica Blue that any one of the four boats could take
victory. He'd seen it before in this very race: in 1997–98
aboard Chessie Racing they had missed second place by

just 50 seconds, when almost the entire fleet had raced
their way from Sydney Heads to a dramatic finish off the
Opera House.

Swain had grown up in the seventies when sailing
was a popular sport amongst white South Africans. And he
was very successful, winning national championships in the
Optimist against 140 boats. But back then, in the apartheid
era, the route to the world stage was very different to that of
his contemporaries racing in Spain, Britain or the USA. Swain
could travel and compete in World Championships on his
English passport, but the Olympics were out of reach.
That simple fact had driven him abroad and into a career
racing big boats. Now the tactical sailing experience of
his youth was about to become useful once again.

In the gathering darkness the quartet paired off:
Blue found themselves match racing Ericsson 3, while
PUMA and Ericsson 4 took a line a little more offshore. It
was important not to focus entirely on the opposition –
there were shoals to navigate and unlit fishing boats to
dodge. They saw the black thundercloud coming, but
were unsure if it would bring wind, rain or both. It was
both, with a violent shift in wind direction and a
doubling in wind speed to 20 knots. Wildly accelerating,
but in the wrong direction, Swain called for a quick gybe
to get them back on course, firing up the generator to
power the keel hydraulics.

As he turned the wheel into the manoeuvre he hit
the keel button, completing a 24-volt circuit through the
eight metres of cable that ran below to the generator.
Instantly, 300 amps of current pulsed into the pump.
Twenty-five litres of hydraulic oil started flowing
through the 38-millimetre hose, to press on to the
piston of a stainless-steel ram. Pascal's principle of

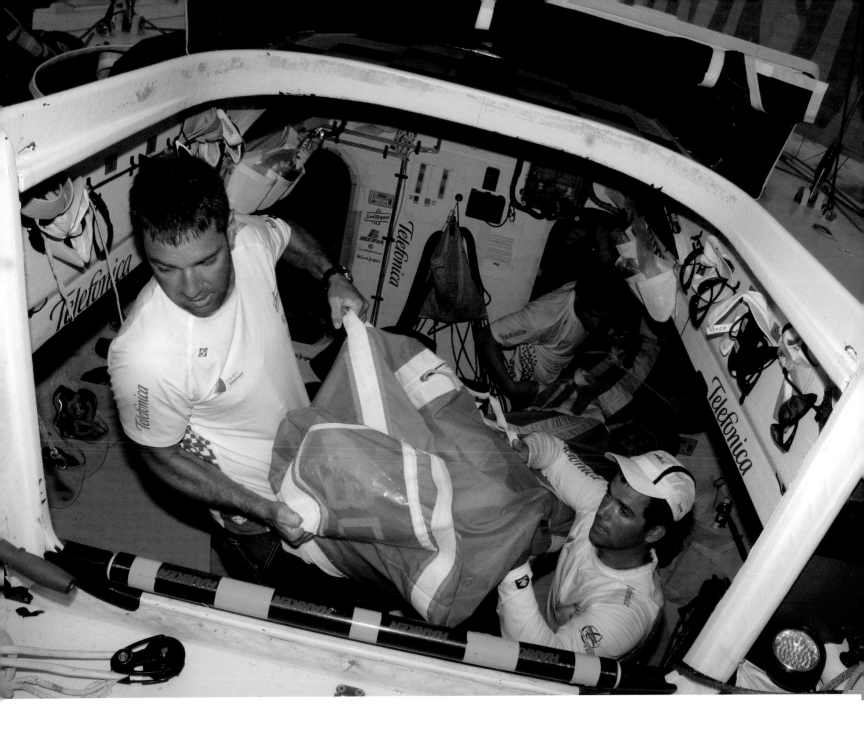

equal pressure in a confined fluid kicked in, and the hydraulic ram translated the moving oil into a force of 72 tonnes at the top of the canting keel. Around the massive, 130-millimetre-thick keel-pin, stainless-steel bearings smoothly began to roll. And below the surface of the Malacca Strait, on the end of 3.5 metres of high-tensile, forged steel keel-fin, 5.6 tonnes of lead bulb began its ponderous, silent swing through the water.

On deck, the short-handed crew wrestled the sails under control on the new gybe, but that was only the start. Everything had been moved forward to get the yacht to take up her most efficient shape for the light air, lifting the wide, flat stern out of the water. Now they were pressed by 20 knots of wind and all the gear had to come into the back of the boat, and be stacked on the windward side to lift the bow and keep the boat flat. Stacking nets were set up on the port side to hold everything to windward, and then, in 25˚C (77˚F) heat and close to 100 per cent humidity, the load hauling started.

First came the 15 plastic toggle bags, colour-coded and filled with the gear they needed for the 10 days at sea: spare ropes and hardware, boatbuilding kit, furling mechanism for the headsails, lifejackets, survival suits and sewing machine. Next there were the food bags, one for every two days, each weighing 22 kilograms. Then the personal bags, 11 in total. Down the boat they went, hand to hand, past the mast and keel structure, on through the galley, and past the companionway, the navigation station and media desk, finally wrenched through the aft waterproof bulkhead doorway and into the stern.

Meanwhile, up above, back on course with the sails trimmed, the sail stack had to be moved. Almost every sail was stored on deck, its position regularly adjusted so that its weight was in the most efficient place for the conditions. Now, the 1.2-tonne stack also had to come aft and to windward. Swain made quick-fire decisions in an attempt to get the sails they were most likely to need next on the top. Ratchet straps were loosened and the sails hauled aft, everything sodden with the rain and about 20 per cent heavier as a result; tired men struggling to be careful of the gear and each other, before the whole lot could finally be strapped down again.

By sunrise, they had clawed a lead of some 50 metres out of Ericsson 3, with PUMA and Ericsson 4 a mile further back. But rounding a tiny headland into an idyllic bay they came to another grinding halt, as the wind died and a foul tide built. PUMA and Ericsson 4 sailed right up to them and put their anchors down. They waited. Telefónica Blue and Ericsson 3 got a little puff and slid offshore, only to see the others pull up their anchors and start to gain. Bekking took them back towards the beach, and battle resumed.

Telefónica Blue would repeat the gybe 12 times down a narrow channel of wind – closer to the land than Ericsson 3, further offshore than Ericsson 4 and PUMA. But the effort paid off; they eked out a 100-metre lead, and crept into a new, northerly breeze. Their lead doubled, and doubled again. The five-knot wind became a 20-knot squall, then a five-knot zephyr. Fishing boats criss-crossed their path. They dodged logs and whole trees in the water, tugs towing barges, and more shipping than anyone had ever imagined. But all the time, Singapore was getting closer. And closer.

Telefónica Blue finally crossed the line to take first place, in darkness, late on 22 December. PUMA followed

right **Quiet conditions at dawn aboard Delta Lloyd, and a good opportunity to have a look around the boat and check that nothing is chafing, fraying, or otherwise out of place. The good crews are constantly attentive to the boat.**

overleaf **Telefónica Black approaches the finish at night in Singapore. Either the fractional zero or the code zero is hoisted; both are attached at the bowsprit and extend almost to the stern of the boat. The only difference is that the fractional zero doesn't hoist all the way to the top of the mast, whereas the code zero does.**

just 17 minutes behind them, with Ericsson 3 less than two minutes away, taking the final place on the podium and getting the better of her sister ship by a mere 40 seconds. The results closed the overall points up. But it was only temporary: Torben Grael and Ericsson 4 took maximum points on a blustery day for the Singapore in-port racing. Telefónica Blue was in third behind PUMA on the day, and that left Ericsson 4 with a 5.5 point overall lead from Bekking and his men, with PUMA just 2.5 points back in third.

Behind this desperate struggle for places on the podium, Telefónica Black had taken a solid fifth, with Green Dragon fending off Team Russia all the way to the line to take sixth. For Jeremy Elliott aboard Team Russia, there was the consolation of knowing that they had been in the race, not watching it. Once finished, they still had a couple of hours of motoring before they could tie up at the ONE°15 Marina on Sentosa Island. When the sails were down and the deck cleared, Team Russia's skipper, Andreas Hanakamp, took the opportunity to call the crew together and tell them that the team was to suspend racing, and would not contest leg four to Qingdao.

Elliott was not surprised; they had been aware for some time that the team's backer, Oleg Zherebtsov, had come under tremendous financial strain as a result of the crisis in world markets. The team had looked for a sponsor to take on the campaign, but these were not good times to be securing multimillion-dollar sponsorships. The time limit for a miracle had expired. They were on death row, though not yet facing the guillotine.

left Martin Krite prepares for a sail change on Ericsson 3 as they chase PUMA and, just visible to the right of the island, Telefónica Blue to the finish in Singapore, 70 miles away. This leg produced one of the tightest finishes the race had ever seen, with the first four all arriving within 20 minutes of each other after 1,950 miles.

And so once again real life had intruded. The Volvo Ocean Race would go on to China with seven boats, not eight, but Team Russia was the victim of market collapse rather than pirates or terrorists. And Roger Nilson, who had sailed the leg in the shadow of the temple tragedy, was pleased to report that "... *the risks of pirates had been, at least in my mind, slightly exaggerated!*"

A few days later, Team Russia departed Sentosa Island for Cape Town under the watchful gaze of the Merlion, the purple statue 37 metres (120 feet) tall – the not-so-mythical symbol of Singapore invented by the tourist board in 1964. Hanakamp would continue his search for sponsorship to enable them to rejoin the race in Rio, Boston or even Galway. But, flying back to Europe with his new fiancée, Jo, to visit his parents in Ireland, Jeremy Elliott was far from confident that Hanakamp would succeed, or even that the team would come back together if he did. None of them could afford to sit and wait to see what happened; jobs had to be found – there were mortgages and, in Elliott's case, a wedding to be paid for. Professional sailing means just that. It has to pay the bills, the same as jobs do in real life.

"Here be Dragons": so ran the warning to medieval mariners intent on voyaging to the east coast of China. And as the Volvo Ocean Race crews surveyed the challenges of leg four from the tropical comfort of Singapore, it still seemed frighteningly relevant. The 2,500 miles north to Qingdao would take them into the domain of the Dragon Kings, the mythical rulers of China's four seas. Through unmarked shoals, freezing winds and notoriously rough water, it was not a journey for the faint of heart.

So there was more tension than usual amongst those saying goodbye to loved ones on the docks of the One°15 Marina, on the morning of 18 January. PUMA's media crew, Rick Deppe, wrote as they motored out to the start:

"I hate the scene at the dock, it's almost too hard to bear sometimes and this one was particularly hard ... It takes a while to get that picture in your head of them [his family] standing on the dock, and put it in a place for later when you need it. It's looking as though the trip could be an interesting one to say the least, definitely a step into the unknown for all of us, and there is a very different mood around the fleet."

It started placidly enough: a perfect 15 knots of wind on a hot, sunny day, with Ericsson 4 and PUMA leading the way out of the Singapore Strait and into the South China Sea. Just as in leg three, the weather would be controlled by the northeast monsoon. The crews settled into the upwind sailing mode that would dominate their existence all the way to Qingdao. The boats fell into single file as the navigators and skippers concurred on the strategy: head for Brunei. Little did they suspect

that the Dragon Kings were just herding them into a corner ready for their first challenge.

The Spratly Islands comprise a group of over 100 small reefs and islets, with a total area of less than five square kilometres. Unfortunately, those five square kilometres are thinly spread over 410,000 square kilometres of the central South China Sea. They are largely uninhabited – except for the military personnel of the various countries that claim sovereignty – and mostly unsurveyed, with charts and sailing directions littered with unhelpful phrases like "Dangerous Ground". The worst area was in the northeast of the islands and, by the evening of 21 January, it was squarely between the boats and Qingdao.

As the sun dipped below the horizon, the fleet split. Five boats took the more treacherous western route: round the worst of the "Dangerous Ground", but still through the islands. It offered a stronger wind, fewer miles, but a dark and seemingly endless night for those navigators and skippers shouldering the responsibility. There were depth gauges that jumped from reading 100 metres to just three. Reefs were four times the size that was marked on the chart, or simply not marked at all. And in the darkness, no one saw anything, even though on occasions the land was close enough to smell. Nonetheless, as the sun rose and the Spratly Islands fell behind them, there were still five boats racing north.

The other two, Ericsson 4 and (after some prevarication) Ericsson 3, had chosen the more conservative, eastern route through the Palawan Passage, which kept them clear of the reefs and shoals. However, while it offered a potentially advantageous,

chapter opener **The epic cityscape of Qingdao at night .**

left **Leg four to Qingdao had the potential to be one of the toughest in the race's history, and there were plenty of anxious people the day of the start in Singapore. They were right to be concerned.**

overleaf **The start of each leg involved a short lap around an inshore course before the fleet headed out to sea. Aboard PUMA (right), the crew are pulling the sails up from down below, where they were stored out of the way for the inshore lap. Aboard Ericsson 3 (left), the crew are seen with the** sails already stacked to windward, where they provide a performance advantage. Although the boats were from different designers, notice the similar layout of the deck equipment; the Telefónica boats were the most innovative in this regard.

right **The crew of PUMA prepare to drop the mainsail after their boom broke in extreme conditions in the Luzon Strait. They subsequently retreated to shelter by the island of Luzon until conditions had moderated. However, they followed the lead that Green Dragon had set in leg two and finished without repairing the boom.**

more easterly wind direction, it was also much closer to the island of Palawan. The influence of the land meant that there was a threat of lighter, more confused breeze – and, unfortunately, that threat was realised. When the fleet converged again north of the Spratly Islands, the two Ericsson boats found themselves in an unfamiliar position: at the back, with a deficit of almost five hours to the leading group of Telefónica Blue, PUMA and Telefónica Black.

For several days, the forecasts had been predicting a storm, and as the leaders continued north, conditions began to deteriorate. But it wasn't until the sun rose on the morning of 24 January, revealing a heaving, grey and white-flecked sea, that Telefónica Blue's watch captain, Jonathan Swain, realised quite how rough it had become. They were west of the Philippine island of Luzon, so they headed inshore where the seas were calmer, but relief was short-lived. Luzon could only provide shelter from the howling northeasterly monsoon wind for so long. Soon they would reach the northern tip, where they could go on, or wait in shelter and lose their lead.

The Kuroshio, or Black Tide, is a notorious warm water current that flows northwards from the Luzon Strait, past Taiwan and on towards Japan. In January it struggles against the northeast monsoon wind which blows at 30 knots or more on an average of one day in every three, but which, on this particular day, happened to be gusting in excess of 50 knots. The result was the same as it is anywhere that wind fights current, from the Needles Channel to the Agulhas Bank: extremely rough water. But Swain recalled afterwards that there

was no committee meeting aboard Telefónica Blue. And even though skipper Bouwe Bekking was prostrate in a bunk after tearing a muscle (he damaged it hurling gear across the boat during a tack), he was adamant. They were going to go on: out into the storm.

The other skippers felt no less compelled to follow – while there was a race, they would sail. One after another they ventured into the Luzon Strait. PUMA was the first to suffer: she snapped her boom in much the same place as Green Dragon had on leg two. Skipper Ken Read turned his boat downwind and sought shelter, and once again PUMA's shore manager, Neil Cox, got busy on the phone. About six hours later, Gerd-Jan Poortman found himself hauling down a badly ripped mainsail with his team-mates, and Delta Lloyd turned back towards shelter to repair it. Less than an hour after that, Green Dragon followed. A structural frame in the bow had shattered. Engineer Tom Braidwood finally had something to fix, though he wasn't the slightest bit happy about it.

Meanwhile, Telefónica Black's navigator, Roger Nilson, had guided them into the shelter of a small bay to change their mainsail for the much smaller storm trysail. Once that was done they set off into the strait. It made no difference. Two hours after they left the shelter of the Luzon coast, Telefónica Black came off a wave and landed with an apocalyptic bang. They immediately turned the boat downwind, and started looking for the damage. When they found it, it was clear that they were going no further without repairs. A substantial crack had opened in the hull. They kept sailing downwind, while Nilson contacted the Race Office and his shore crew.

Still at the back of the fleet, the crews aboard Ericsson 4 and Ericsson 3 had been able to watch as one boat after another had been picked off. Ericsson 4's watch captain, Stu Bannatyne, related afterwards that they had talked about waiting, even before Telefónica Blue had pushed on. So when the carnage started, it was an easy decision to haul down the mainsail and jog slowly up the coast with just the storm jib up, tracking behind their sister ship, who had adopted the same approach.

Bannatyne explained their strategy. Ever since the team's American meteorologist, Chris Bedford, had done their original study of the new course, they had known that this leg was potentially the most hazardous the race had ever embarked on. They also knew that while they were unlikely to secure a race-winning points margin on the way to Qingdao, they could potentially damage the boat so badly that they would be unable to start the leg to Rio, which would lose them any chance of the overall prize. So when they won the in-port race in Singapore and further extended their lead, the decision was confirmed: getting to Qingdao was the absolute priority; they would happily accept a third or fourth place to ensure that they made it.

Seven boats had sailed up the coast of Luzon on the morning of 24 January; just five boats had ventured out into the strait. And by the time a spectacular blue sky darkened to the blackest of nights, only one of them was still going. From the wheel of Telefónica Blue, the only thing visible to Jonathan Swain was the white of the huge breaking crests bearing down on them. The instruments recorded waves over 14 metres high, the height of a three-storey building. The anemometer had

above Ericsson 3's helmsman (left) has nowhere to hide if he's going to keep holding on to the wheel. The situation isn't much better for the man at the winch-grinding pedestal aboard Telefónica Blue (right). When everyone was in their normal sailing positions, these were usually the two most exposed jobs.

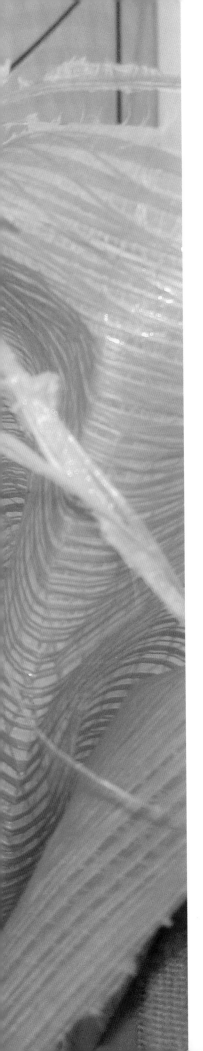

topped out at a wind speed of 55 knots before disintegrating. But getting through those initial hours proved crucial; as they learned the lessons, their chances of survival rapidly increased. Now they had the correct balance of sail area – three reefs in the mainsail and a storm jib – giving just enough speed to steer around the worst of the breaking crests, but not so much that they flew off the backs of the waves and became dangerously airborne.

They learned to cant the keel the wrong way, forcing the boat to heel more than it would have otherwise, so that when it did take off it landed on soft curves and not the flat bottom. The stack of sails was no longer required to help keep the boat upright, so they hauled them down below, safe from the walls of grey water washing down the deck. The daggerboards were pulled up a little to let the boat slide sideways more, going with the flow, rather than fighting the storm's energy. Wedged into his bunk, Bekking was feeling every wave, and wrote: *"In these conditions, down below is the best way to feel how big the crashes are, and when to throttle back."* A couple of times, Bekking stepped in to stop them from putting up bigger sails. But it was Swain and co-skipper, Spanish Olympic gold medallist Iker Martínez, who bore the brunt of the responsibility for keeping the boat in one piece as they negotiated one ugly wave after another.

While Swain and those with him battled to keep their boat together, the battering that the rest of the fleet had taken meant that there was little pressure on Ericsson 4 to follow, particularly when the weather forecast was predicting a shift in wind direction that would give them every opportunity to catch up. They continued to "mill around in the darkness", as Bannatyne put it later, occasionally venturing four or five miles from the coast to check that conditions hadn't changed. Then, six hours after Telefónica Black had turned back from the strait, Ericsson 3 set off. Aboard Ericsson 4, they elected to wait to see how they fared. Three hours later, their team-mates on the sister ship were still headed north. Only now did Ericsson 4 follow.

Since Green Dragon had established that the boat could be sailed without the boom in leg two, the crew of PUMA weren't trying to fix it. They, like Ericsson 4, were waiting for the weather. Even before the storm had struck, Rick Deppe had filmed a media report in which Ken Read had said that it might be possible to wait for as long as a day and still get to Qingdao at the same time as if they had sailed straight on. Now, PUMA took advantage of that analysis, leaving the shelter of Luzon in fourth place, just a couple of hours after Ericsson 4, but from a bay much further south. She was 200 miles behind Telefónica Blue.

That choice wasn't available to Green Dragon, with the damage to her structural frame in the bow. The crew had conferred with their engineers while sailing back towards Luzon, and Tom Braidwood had a plan formed by the time they arrived in Salomague Bay. There they found Delta Lloyd, already anchored in the darkness, her crew repairing their mainsail and a broken steering wheel. Initially Braidwood enlisted the help of his watch captain Neal McDonald, and Irish bowman, Justin Slattery.

McDonald made use of his first-class honours degree in engineering science and his MSc in naval

left Delta Lloyd seeks shelter from the storm in Salomague Bay to undergo repairs. The damaged mainsail is visible, and Martin Watts lowers the much smaller storm trysail that they have used to retreat to a safe anchorage.

left While the main work on Green Dragon was the structural repair to the bow, there was also some sail damage to be fixed. Sailmaker Phil Harmer works in the sunshine just outside the main hatch.

right Tom Braidwood (centre) organises the repair team aboard Green Dragon at the anchorage in Salomague Bay: Phil Harmer (bottom right), Justin Slattery (top left) and Neal McDonald (top right). They are mixing resin, soaking it into strips of carbon fibre and rolling and painting them into place to reinforce the damaged structure.

right   Delta Lloyd arrives in Taiwan with sails, sail bags, foul-weather clothing, safety harnesses and lifejackets spread out to dry. She subsequently retired from the leg because of the damage sustained and was shipped to Rio de Janeiro, via Hong Kong, aboard a German freighter. Arriving in Rio, she was repaired by her original builder, Killian Bushe, who also built Ericsson 3 and 4.

Depending on the length of the leg, and what food, sails, spares and other supplies were carried, the equipment added to the boat could weigh well in excess of two tonnes. The rules stipulated that the weight of the boat when empty should be between 13,860 and 14,000 kilograms.

architecture on a long, tedious night of manual labour with hacksaws and sandpaper. It was a job that would have taken a fraction of the time with the right power tools, so they were all relieved when they finally got to the stage of laminating the new structure into place. In all, they added about four kilograms of resin and fibre to the bow. And it was well into the morning when McDonald finally went up on deck and discovered what he later described as "the best anchorage in the world". The storm still raged in the distance, but all he could see of it was some rustling in the tops of the palm trees. Around him the water was calm, the sunshine hot and bright. It was a beautiful day in paradise.

They wouldn't be hanging around to enjoy it; everyone on Green Dragon felt the pressure to get to Qingdao. They had several Chinese sponsors, and it was home to their media crew, Guo Chuan. And the boat had been built in China, at the McConaghy factory in Zuhui. As the team's project manager, Tom Braidwood had taken his family to live there with him, although he had barely seen them for six months, what with working 16-hour days to get finished on time. But now, if they could get to the mainland, it would make a final repair that much easier, as a new frame could be trucked up from the factory.

Green Dragon returned to the race a little more than 24 hours after suffering the damage. Delta Lloyd followed her out of Salomague Bay less than half an hour later. McDonald commented afterwards that the Green Dragon crew had "raised the 'no-heroes' flag" and were doing everything they could to nurse their boat home without damaging the primary structure of the hull panels. Unfortunately, they weren't quite gentle

enough. Green Dragon's bulkhead cracked again, above the original repair, and Tom Braidwood went back to work even as they struggled onwards. Delta Lloyd had no such problems and quickly passed them, pushing harder into what were still big seas, accompanied by 35 knots of wind.

Both boats, however, were better off than Telefónica Black, who had motored further south to Subic Bay to meet members of her shore crew. After assessing the damage, the boat returned to Singapore. From there, she was eventually shipped to Rio de Janeiro, where a team of boatbuilders readied her to rejoin the race for leg six, giving up all the points available from leg four, the Qingdao in-port race, and leg five with its two scoring gates. It was exactly the nightmare scenario that Bannatyne and his colleagues aboard Ericsson 4 dreaded.

All the skippers were wrestling with the same issues of responsibility – but it was Green Dragon's Ian Walker that captured them most eloquently in an email written while they battled their way to Qingdao in their damaged boat:

"The helmsman had a near impossible task to try and steer around waves he couldn't see, but could maybe sense or feel. For those down below they had to listen to the crashing and banging and endure the terrible moments when you feel the boat go up in the air and you are waiting to see how hard it lands.

Lying in a bunk is hard enough, sleeping next to impossible. I couldn't rest, spending much of my time up in the bow monitoring the repair and any flexing of the bow panels. This has been my biggest challenge ever as a skipper. The responsibility of the boat, the programme,

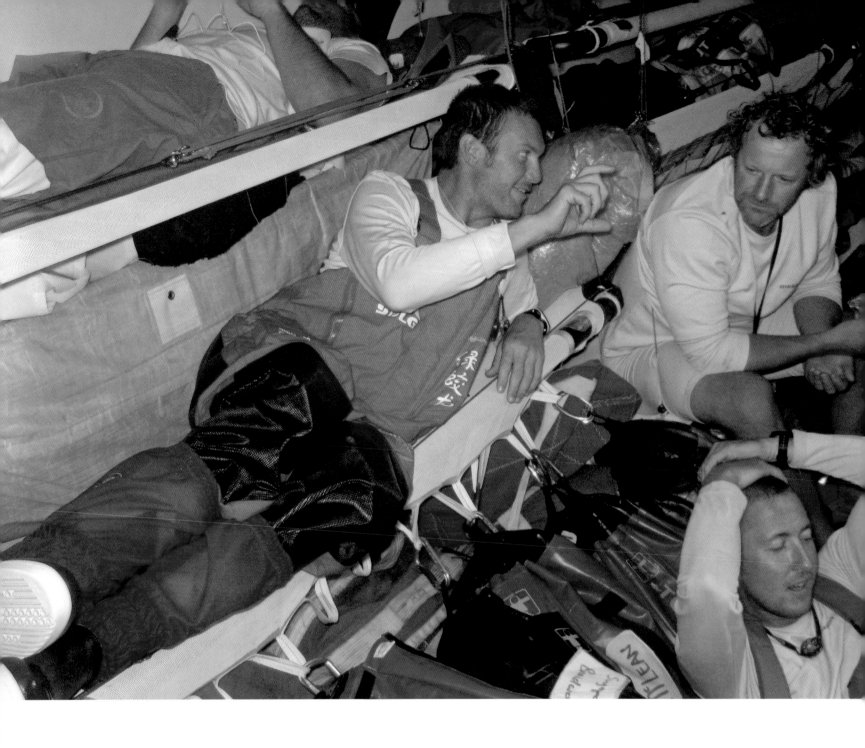

above The Green Dragon crew get some respite from the battle up on deck: top bunk, Tom Braidwood; below him, Phil Harmer and Andrew McLean; with Neal McDonald to the right. Conditions below are hot and cramped at the best of times; cold, wet and squalid at the worst. For the high-latitude legs, several crews took blow-up mattresses to go between the sleeping bag and the bunk. It provided some comfort and insulation, as the bunk is normally just a construction of plastic mesh suspended from a four-sided frame, hinged off the hull.

the sponsors and, of course, potentially the lives of those on board rest in your hands and decisions.
Should we stop and let conditions abate? Should we press on? How fast should we go? What are the wind and waves going to do? Which route should we take to get most shelter? How much punishment can the boat take? Are we doing the right thing?"

Meanwhile, those at the front of the fleet, several hundred miles further north, reached lighter winds off the east coast of Taiwan. But it wasn't over yet; the Dragon Kings had one final test before they would let them escape the Kuroshio. A heaving swell was the clue. There was breeze somewhere, and it turned out that it was just around the corner from the northern tip of Taiwan. Telefónica Blue hit it first, and Jonathan Swain could only reflect afterwards on how fortunate they had been that it was daylight and they could see the change coming. Within minutes they were sailing under just the storm jib again, with the mainsail lashed to the boom.

Behind them in second place, Ericsson 3 wasn't quite so fortunate. They had already had to repair their mainsail once, and when this second storm hit, the sail split again. All hands were called on deck to take it down and get it below to where the sailmakers were setting up the sewing machine. Bowman Martin Krite was sitting on the boom to wrestle the sail free of the mast when the word came up from below: "We're taking on water." Those are words no one ever wants to hear on a yacht, but particularly a yacht already hard-pressed in a storm. Immediately, they turned downwind, and while the others secured the mainsail, the watch captain, New Zealand veteran Richard Mason, went below to have a look.

When he opened the door to the forward watertight compartment, a grim tide spilled out. Ten days of rubbish had been stored in the bow in plastic bags that had now burst. A filthy, knee-deep morass of food wrappings, baby wipes and other human detritus flowed aft. Mason and the boat captain, Jens Dolmer, pushed their way into the pitch-black stink of the forward compartment to try and locate the hull fissure. Disgusting as they were, the smell and the instant squalor weren't the problem. The rest of the crew had to bail the water out, but there was no chance of the pumps working for more than a few seconds at a time, because all the rubbish swilling around would have instantly clogged the filters.

Martin Krite and his mates set to with the buckets, but it was a losing battle. The water came in a lot faster than they could bail it out. The emergency grab-bags were hauled out of the lockers, along with the survival suits. Then, inspiration: they tore the plastic mesh holdall that the kitchen utensils were stored in off the bulkhead and put the pump inside it. It worked; safe from the rubbish, the pumps started to help the men with buckets hold back the sea, until finally they found the hole. It looked to have been punched upwards from the outside, as though they had crashed into something hard floating in the water. Mason stuck his boot into the gap and slowed the flow right down, while Krite and the others kept bailing. Slowly, the water came under control. The lid was cut off the engine box and, when the water was almost gone, a section was stuck over the hole with waterproof glue.

A short examination told them they weren't safe yet. A large area of the carbon-fibre hull panel was

left Ericsson 3 is transported on a barge from Keelung, where she arrived in Taiwan and was first hoisted out of the water for damage inspection, to Hualien, where she was repaired. It was a rare chance to see the boat with both daggerboards and rudders in place – one for the design geeks.

top right In the Hualien workshop, the new, replacement hull panel is raised into place on Ericsson 3 to test the fit. The extent of the damage is clear from the area of hull that is being repaired.

bottom right The replacement panel used in the Ericsson 3 repair was actually constructed in Italy and then flown out to Taiwan, where it was fitted to the carefully prepared hull. The boat arrived in Taiwan just after noon GMT on 27 January, and restarted leg four just before midnight GMT on 11 February.

cracked, and had separated from the layer underneath. The whole hull was moving about 15 centimetres as they surged over the waves. Krite and the others started pulling the bunks apart, so they could use the pieces to brace the weakening structure. And no one needed to tell them that they wouldn't be taking any further part in the race to Qingdao for a while. The boat steered a course for Keelung in the northeast of Taiwan, which was thankfully close. But it was only when they sighted a coastguard ship, out to accompany them for the final miles, that they knew they were safe.

The news of Ericsson 3 turning for Taiwan sent a ripple of anxiousness through the crew of Ericsson 4. They didn't know what had happened, and they were sailing a boat of the same design, built by the same people. Their storm jib had already pulled a fixing off the deck. Boat captain David Endean and three others had repaired it – one doing the work above deck, one below, with two more to hold them in place in the seaway. After they got the news of their sister ship, Endean checked the hull again – but could find no other damage.

Delta Lloyd wasn't so fortunate. As the new storm ripped south and delivered the fleet its second pasting in a handful of days, they too found trouble in the bow structure. It was not as dramatic as the punctured hull of Ericsson 3, but Gerd-Jan Poortman and his team-mates couldn't go on either. They joined Ericsson 3, sheltering in Keelung. From there, the boat was subsequently shipped to Rio de Janeiro for repair, to rejoin the race in leg six, along with Telefónica Black. There were now just four boats left on the water, and one of them, Green Dragon, had already acknowledged that she was more

left Telefónica Blue arrives triumphant in Qingdao, just ahead of a bank of fog that obscured the finish for spectators, sailors and race officials. While skipper Bouwe Bekking's decision to sail on into the storm had been vindicated after an extraordinary display of seamanship, for others, discretion had been the better part of valour.

above **The arrival ceremony in Qingdao was spectacular. And for many of the crews and shore teams, used to the old race route, or the European, North American or Australasian sailing circuits,** the culture shock continued for the whole stopover, just as it had in India.

concerned about getting to Qingdao than trying to overtake anyone.

But as Telefónica Blue, Ericsson 4 and PUMA clawed their way out of the Kuroshio and its waves, the wind finally started to moderate. It also began to shift as forecast and, at every turn, it brought the chasing boats closer. On the final leg up the Yellow Sea, PUMA passed Ericsson 4 as her crew struggled to clear themselves from a fishing net. She got to within an hour and a quarter of Telefónica Blue, but had to settle for second place, with Ericsson 4 third. Neal McDonald, Tom Braidwood, Ian Walker and the rest of the crew eventually nursed their wounded Dragon home in fourth, arriving to a rapturous welcome in Qingdao, a couple of days after the others. Afterwards, McDonald commented, "They could all have got here, if they had gone slow enough." He neatly captured the challenge that leg four had presented as none of the others had: how to balance the demands of seamanship with the urge to race.

It took a monumental effort by her shore crew, but Green Dragon was ready for the in-port race, which, ironically, was then delayed two days waiting for sufficient wind. When the breeze finally arrived, the four-boat fleet finished in exactly the same order as they held on the overall table: Ericsson 4, Telefónica Blue, PUMA and Green Dragon. The points were then further adjusted when Telefónica Blue took the three-point penalty to enable her to change her rudders for the rest of the race. So the position going into leg five was Ericsson 4 with a seven-point lead from Blue in second place, who was just one point ahead of PUMA.

But leg four wasn't quite over. The Ericsson team put a massive effort into Ericsson 3, building a new hull panel in Italy and shipping it to Taiwan, where the yacht was repaired. After days of 24/7 struggle by the team, they resumed racing on 11 February, just before midnight. They finished a little over 58 hours later, picking up four points for fifth place. Unfortunately, that was five hours after the start of leg five. The team had been preparing the pit-stop for days, and there was no time for any human comforts – no showers or shaves. Twenty of the shore crew flooded on to the boat, each with a specific task – bigger fuel tanks were fitted for this extra long leg; the mainsail and some running rigging were changed; food was loaded and stored down below. A long list of small jobs was carefully worked through; everything was ticked off. The boat was tied up to the dock in Qingdao for just 55 minutes, after which she headed back out to start leg five. And so, for Ericsson 3, one leg blended seamlessly into another.

Forty Days

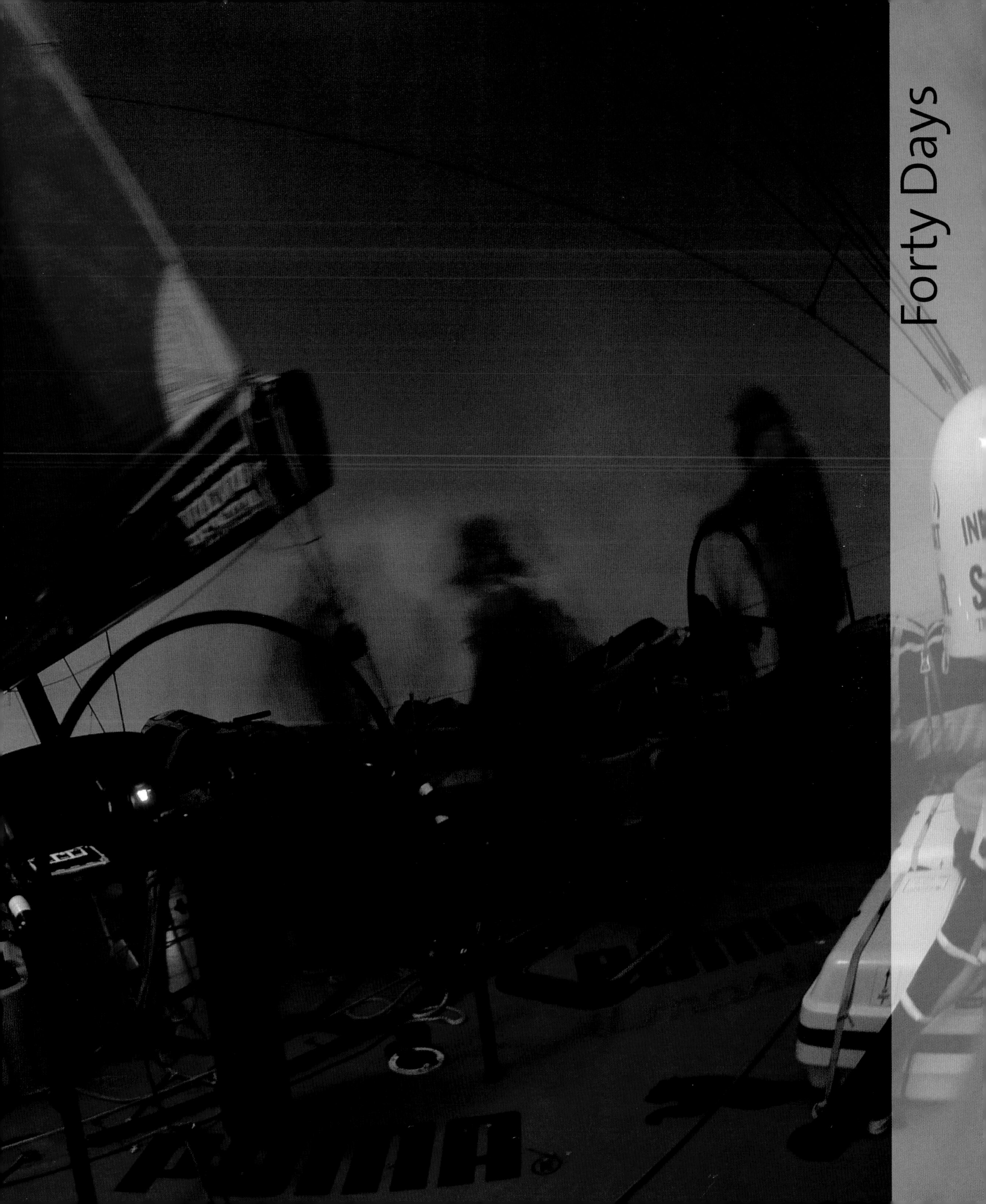

chapter opener PUMA glides through the Pacific at night.

left Although they spend a lot of time down below, the relatively small number of crew on the Volvo Open 70 means that the navigators all have to get involved in crew work. Jules Salter (facing camera) gets his hands dirty aboard Ericsson 4.

It is almost a tradition. In every Volvo Ocean Race navigators fall like cherry blossom in spring. And, unlike the crew on deck, it is rarely because they are injured. The pressure of the job is immense; hardly a surprise given that it involves analysing, interpreting and gambling on something as fickle as the weather. This time around it was no different. By the start of leg five in Qingdao, two of the eight navigators who had sailed from Alicante had been edged off their perches.

American Matt Gregory had left Delta Lloyd in Singapore, eventually being replaced by Team Russia's Wouter Verbraak. Then, in China, Telefónica Blue's starting navigator, Simon Fisher, was moved sideways. Fisher joined the crew on deck, while one of the team's meteorologists, Australian Tom Addis, moved into the still-warm seat below. It was a 25 per cent attrition rate. So imagine the pressure on 40-year-old Englishman Jules Salter, navigator of the overall leader, Ericsson 4.

Ericsson 4 had a significant advantage in points. They were regarded as having equal or superior speed to most boats, in most conditions. Surely only a major tactical blunder or serious equipment failure could stop them winning overall? But if there were any tactical blunders to be made and blame apportioned, Salter was a lot more likely to find himself in the firing line than his garlanded skipper, Torben Grael.

Leaving Qingdao, Salter had no simple task. It was a 12,300-mile odyssey down the Yellow Sea, across the Pacific, from the northern to the southern hemisphere, from winter to summer, with New Zealand to starboard and Cape Horn to port, before they could even think about the final 2,000 miles up the South American coast to the leg's finish line in Rio de Janeiro. Leg five was

the longest leg the race had ever seen, and it was worth the most points with two scoring gates: one for the first boat to cross the line of latitude at 36 deg S, and the other at Cape Horn. By the time it was done, over half the overall points would have been awarded. Leg five had all the makings of a tipping point – a make-or-break, race-defining moment.

Jules Salter grew up surrounded by professional sailing. He was brought up in Cowes on the Isle of Wight, the southern limit of England's Solent, going to school there during the 1970s and 1980s. It was a period when those waters were a focus for the nascent world of modern professional sailing, during the quadrennial Whitbread Race and the biennial Admiral's Cup and Fastnet Race. He was introduced to the sport by his father, via that archetypal home-built kit boat, the Mirror. And he was soon going sailing with anyone who would take him from the unpretentious club at Gurnard, where the family were members.

The background of the Solent provided plenty of inspiration – he was late to school the day that UBS charged past his house to win line honours in the 1985–86 Whitbread Race. But by the time Salter had abandoned a legal career to become a professional sailor and risen through the ranks to do his first Volvo Ocean Race (with second-placed Pirates of the Caribbean in 2005–06), the race neither started nor finished anywhere near the Solent.

If the previous race had broken new ground when it began in Spain, then the 2008–09 event really turned the format on its head, dropping the old clipper ship trading route through the Southern Ocean, with stops in New Zealand or Australia, in favour of sailing around

right Only PUMA, Green Dragon and Ericsson 4 started together, racing along the waterfront in Qingdao before heading out into the Yellow Sea. While leg five started slowly, it didn't take long for the wind to pick up.

the southern boundaries of Asia. Initially, the impact of the change was felt most dramatically by the navigators and their support teams. In Salter's case, that meant bespectacled American meteorologist (and licensed pilot) Chris Bedford, and the Whitbread-winning New Zealand navigator Mike Quilter. They had to research entirely new areas of the planet, places that hadn't seen truly hard-pressed sailing boats since the days of the square riggers.

The team developed a system for planning each of the race legs. Chris Bedford had a set of computer weather data that went back 30 years. This could be modified to take account of the varying influence of events like El Niño, which can have a dramatic impact on the weather in the Pacific. Using this data, Bedford then developed a set of three potential routes for each leg, each one being the fastest for a common pattern of weather, e.g. low-pressure systems moving along a particular path; a high pressure sitting in a regular position; and so on.

Meanwhile, armed with his own vast experience, Mike Quilter's task was to research the non-computerised sources of sailing wisdom such as pilot charts and the accounts of the old square-rigger voyages, bringing to the table as much practical knowledge as possible. Then the team would discuss the pros and cons of each of Bedford's route options, using Quilter's input to look for things that the computer analysis might have missed: for instance, the difference that a bad sea state might make. They would gradually refine their knowledge of each of the options and its risks and advantages in all the likely weather patterns.

right Spanish sailor Jordi Calafat had already won world championships, Olympic gold and the America's Cup before he joined Telefónica Blue for the Volvo Ocean Race.

Fifteen days before the start of each leg, Bedford would then begin to run ensemble modelling. A computerised mathematical algorithm raced a virtual Volvo Open 70 through the weather forecasts of several different meteorological offices. The idea was to try and pick which of the three route options was most likely to be appropriate at start time – a decision usually made with a couple of days to go.

Then it was a process of gradually refining the detail of each part of the plan: what angle to approach a weather system; where was the quickest point to cross an area of light wind; etc. Finally, when the gun went, Salter was completely focused on the fine grain of the picture: what sail and what compass course best executed the plan.

Ericsson 4 wasn't about to make a strategic blunder because of a lack of preparation, and the process had worked demonstrably well for four legs. The team had barely put a tactical foot in the wrong place, and sat atop the leader board with a seven-point lead. The unique problem on leg five was the sheer scale of it. The three optimum routes were potentially 1,000 miles apart. Early decisions had to be made with absolutely no knowledge of how the weather might eventually align to determine the outcome, because the very best long-term forecasts only ran to seven days. Or, as Salter subsequently put it in an email, *"We're trying to line the boats up for weather that hasn't even formed yet."*

When the boats peeled away from the dock in Qingdao at the end of a spectacular Chinese departure ceremony, the most pressing challenge to Ericsson 4's crown was coming from Spain's Telefónica Blue. Skipper Bouwe

Bekking and his team had recorded back-to-back wins on the previous two legs. The pressure was on for another strong performance to continue to close the gap to the leader.

And superstar Spanish helmsman Jordi Calafat knew all about pressure. He had been competing in major regattas since he was 12 years old. That was when he first sailed in the Optimist World Championships, an event he won a year later. At 18, he left school and became a sailmaker. By 24, he had won multiple World Championships in the International 470 Olympic dinghy, and a gold medal at the Barcelona Games in 1992. In 2007, along with former Volvo Ocean Race–winning navigator Juan Vila, he became one of the first Spanish sailors to win the America's Cup.

There were many things that Calafat's vast experience had taught him to anticipate at the start of a 12,300-mile race, on a foggy, calm Qingdao day, but ending up on his backside on the foredeck beside watch captain Jonathan Swain was not one of them. The rig was shaking like a leaf. A moment before, they had been gliding along at five knots, now they were stationary. It lasted only a moment before Telefónica Blue shook herself free, but there was no question that they had hit something.

The unfortunate man with the chart in his hand was the newly installed Tom Addis, but whatever they had hit, it wasn't marked. The closest rock should have been 130 metres away. But that didn't alter the fact that they had hit something, and with less than 20 minutes to the start they had to deal with it. The mainsail was soon on the way back down to the deck. The yacht was rigged with an endoscope, a system for visually checking the keel from inside the boat, normally used to see if she

right Telefónica Blue is hoisted back out of the water after grounding on a rock before the start in Qingdao. There is a very different layout to the deck and cockpit in comparison with PUMA and Ericsson 3 on pages 92 and 93. At the finish, several sailors cited this as an innovation that they would look at for the next race. It allows the stack of sails on the windward side to be lowered and protected by the hull.

was dragging weed. The water was too dirty for it to help. They kept an emergency dive kit on board, and it was passed to the support boat for a swimmer to go down and have a look. Unfortunately, they didn't have a weight belt, and without it, the swimmer couldn't get deep enough to see anything of the critical join between the bulb and the fin. It was an awful decision to have to make, but Calafat agreed with the others – they had to go in and pull the boat out of the water to check it properly.

Just three minutes remained before the starting gun when Telefónica Blue contacted the Race Committee and informed them that, just as on leg one, they would be forced to suspend racing. They returned to the dock to be hoisted out of the water. The initial diagnosis was bad. All the fairing had popped out of the join between the bulb and the fin, there was a big dent in the front of the bulb where they had first hit the rock, and then more damage along the bottom from bumping over it. Fortunately, members of the design team were on hand from Farr Yacht Design. The shore team set about repairing the obvious damage, while a specialist in ultrasound structural testing was brought in from Shanghai to do a complete check.

Once the plan had been established, Bekking gathered the crew and explained the schedule. Calafat, Swain and the others recovered their bags from the air-freight container bound for Rio, returned to the hotel and checked back in. It was the second time they had spent the first night of a leg in a hotel room, rather than at sea. If that wasn't frustrating enough, while the repairs were going on Ericsson 3 arrived from Taiwan, completed leg four, then turned around and headed

back out in front of them. It was a dreadful start to their leg-five challenge for the overall lead.

The early starters had sailed out into a tranquil Yellow Sea, and spent the first 14 hours languishing in light winds. When the wind freshened it did so from the back of the fleet first, the wind arriving from the northeast. It quickly pushed Ericsson 3 to within 30 miles of the leaders, Ericsson 4 and PUMA. It was what the Chinese might have called an auspicious beginning for the Nordic crew. By the time Telefónica Blue left Qingdao 19 hours after the start, the northeasterly breeze blew solidly right across the Yellow Sea, and everyone was moving fast. Telefónica Blue was 150 miles behind the fleet. Calafat told himself that they had plenty of time to catch up. It was his sailing philosophy to be patient, to wait for the opportunities, to let the others make mistakes.

Once the breeze arrived it increased steadily and the fleet ripped past South Korea and the southern tip of Japan, the gusts hitting more than 40 knots as they negotiated the islands and the dozens of fishing boats that worked those waters. The only mishap was a broken steering wheel on PUMA, which there was plenty of time to fix. While the sailing was relentlessly harsh, it was all on port tack, which only required one wheel. They drove the boats on into the building warmth of the northeast trade winds. The spray fired constantly back across the deck, and there were few if any sail changes to break up the pattern. It was a case of stand firm, trim the sails and take the soaking for four hours, then return to the stinking sweat-box below decks to spend another four hours trying to sleep in the heat, as they ate up the miles to the equator.

left Perfect conditions for some high-speed sailing on Ericsson 4. The mainsail is attached to the mast via the 'batten cars'. The battens are mounted horizontally across the mainsail to give it structure and shape. They fasten to the batten cars, which then run on bearings up and down a track on the back edge of the mast.

Jules Salter and his weather team had elected on the middle route out of the three options that they had assessed for the leg. Ericsson 4 was aiming for a point somewhere between Fiji and Vanuatu, and the rest of the fleet seemed happy to follow. She maintained a slight edge over PUMA, whose skipper Ken Read and navigator Andrew Cape had chosen a line a few miles further west. Telefónica Blue followed PUMA, Bekking and Addis still playing the patience game, biding their time, while Ericsson 3 was simply driving down the wake of her sister ship. All those boats were comfortable with the pace, but it was different for Green Dragon.

Skipper Ian Walker and the team were again a touch slow in the breezy reaching conditions. A pattern was emerging, which Walker blamed on the fact that the bulb of Green Dragon's keel was some 500 kilograms lighter than most of the other bulbs. Legendary English yacht-designer Uffa Fox was right when he said that weight is only of use to the designer of a steamroller, but when a yacht is built to a specific overall weight like the Volvo Open 70, as much of it as possible needs to be in the bulb. There it acts against the force of the wind trying to tip the boat over, and at certain sailing angles this so-called righting moment translates into raw speed.

Struggling for pace, Green Dragon's crew was again the first to make a strategic move, gradually easing themselves out to the eastern side of the fleet through the first week. They had consistently been more willing to separate than anyone else, and it had paid dividends for them. The Doldrums crossing on leg one had been the most spectacular example, but there had also been good gains on the first night out of Cape Town

and India. Afterwards, watch captain Neal McDonald would describe the strategy as a willingness to accept separation when it fitted their plan for the weather. They were sailing the route they believed to be fastest, and if that took them away from the fleet, then so be it.

It was a very different matter for Jules Salter aboard Ericsson 4. In sailing, risk is largely measured by the amount of separation between the boats across the race course: specifically, measured at right angles to the route to the finish. Such separation is usually called leverage, with much the same meaning as in finance: the greater the leverage, the greater the risk of gains and losses. Green Dragon's boat-speed problems meant she was willing to accept leverage, but to Jules Salter it was anathema.

Ericsson 4 had the speed to match or better anyone in the fleet in most conditions, and so Salter's principle was simple, what he called "playing the fleet". It was no less dependent on an analysis of the weather, but once he identified where he thought the advantage was, then he, along with skipper Torben Grael, would simply try to position the boat on that side of the fleet. If the advantage was to the east, then being just a single mile further east than the main competition was fine. No more separation was required.

Whatever style of sailing was adopted, it required the ability to make accurate judgements about upcoming conditions. So no one was happy when the fleet hit a black spot for satellite communications, effectively closing the normal routes for receipt of weather information. The boats usually relied on Inmarsat's high bandwidth FleetBroadband system, but Inmarsat was undergoing a well-publicised reshuffle of

its satellite constellation, and was out of use for the first 10 days of the leg. As they closed on the Doldrums, this coincided with the fleet hitting a known blind spot in the coverage of the system they had been using instead, the slower Fleet 33.

Jules Salter and his fellow navigators were forced back on some rather older technology, as Salter reported from the boat:

"Sod's law of course dictates that we are in the 100 nm or so before we enter the first light and fickle Doldrums belt on this voyage ... Much to the amusement of those of a certain age on board, I have got the old school weather fax running ... There is a pleasure in receiving a slightly blurred weather map from the airwaves as you hear the tone come in over the SSB [Single-Side Band] radio. You have to tune the unit, look up a schedule, set up the software and also make sure no one has accidentally pulled the plug out of the backstay antenna as they take a leak off the back of the yacht."

By 22 February, PUMA and Telefónica Blue had joined Ericsson 3 in line astern behind Ericsson 4. Even Green Dragon had closed her leverage down to around 100 miles, and as she was 300 miles behind, that was hardly threatening. Clearly, the collective stomach for risk was weak – good news for Salter. But as they hit the Doldrums that morning, the leaders got the worst of it and Telefónica Blue and Green Dragon both halved their deficits to less than 150 miles. PUMA was the more immediate threat to Salter and Ericsson 4, and her lead of 50 miles dropped to 20 before the leader struggled clear. PUMA's experience was no less chastening, as Ericsson 3 sailed up over the horizon to land right beside them. It was the start of an intense boat-on-boat race that would last five days.

left The crew of Telefónica Blue tidies up after reefing the mainsail. The reef means that the sail has been lowered to decrease its area and make it more manageable. The extra cloth generated by the reef can be seen hanging off the bottom of the boom. Everyone has helmets on in the high-speed conditions, because of the constant spray.

right PUMA (red) and Telefónica Blue (blue) took the western route through the channel between Viti Levu and Vanua Levu, while Ericsson 4 (grey), Ericsson 3 (orange) and Green Dragon (green) went east of the islands. PUMA switched from the eastern option with the latter three, to lead Telefónica Blue through the channel.

But they weren't quite done with the Doldrums, which in this part of the Pacific occurred in a double belt, separated by a band of easterly trade winds. The fleet hit the second belt (technically known as the South Pacific Convergence Zone) on 26 February. And by the time it got moving again, the islands of Fiji were square and centre in the way. Initially, this looked to have played into the hands of Ericsson 4. The calculations now suggested that the fastest route was to the east of the islands, rather than the west, which would force everyone to again fall into line behind them, as they tacked upwind to go around that side. Green Dragon would make big gains, as she was still the most easterly boat, but from Jules Salter's point of view, the real threat overall was from Telefónica Blue and PUMA. And if they were all forced to play follow-the-leader around Fiji, the leverage would reduce to zero and Salter could, momentarily anyway, relax.

Being the most westerly boat at this stage, it looked a particularly grim scenario for Telefónica Blue. But Bekking and Addis had a spectacular solution. They would sail between the main islands of Viti Levu and Vanua Levu, down a badly charted channel strewn with coral reefs. Green Dragon's skipper, Ian Walker, had already declared in an audio interview that he didn't think anyone would "take it on", so the move came as a surprise for racers and spectators alike. Then, on 27 February, PUMA also took it on, peeling away from the side of Ericsson 3 after five days of boat-on-boat racing to blaze a trail down to join Telefónica Blue on her Fijian adventure.

PUMA's move was a nightmare for Salter. Twenty-four hours previously they'd had the situation locked down, and now, suddenly, it was completely out of control. All of the major competition was headed the other way. PUMA and Telefónica Blue were forcing at least 100 miles of leverage. Jules Salter sweated through the calculations one more time ... but they stayed with Plan A. The pair of Ericsson boats joined Green Dragon in beating upwind round the eastern side of the islands, while PUMA and Telefónica Blue struggled through the channel. In his understated style, Salter reported from the boat, "If it's a bad decision then the leg could be over for us ... which would be pretty disappointing."

It hadn't been an easy decision aboard PUMA either. After all, they were the ones who had created the separation. If it went wrong, then Read and Cape might find it difficult to justify to the crew. Amongst that crew for leg five was the American Jerry Kirby, famous for being, at 52, the world's oldest bowman. It was a title he had held for some time; it's widely regarded as a young man's game up at the pointed end.

After sailing leg one to Cape Town, Kirby had gone home to deal with the impact the credit crunch was having on his construction business. To say that the process was ongoing would be an understatement, but not even financial apocalypse, defaulting clients and troublesome employees were going to stop Jerry Kirby from doing leg five. Afterwards he said, "It was really stupid to do this leg, as a businessman."

Kirby is the eternal optimist, famous for his perpetual cheer and a wealth of stories. He had come up through the sport the old way, the hard way. Born in the original home of the America's Cup, Newport, Rhode Island, he had watched his first Cup from his

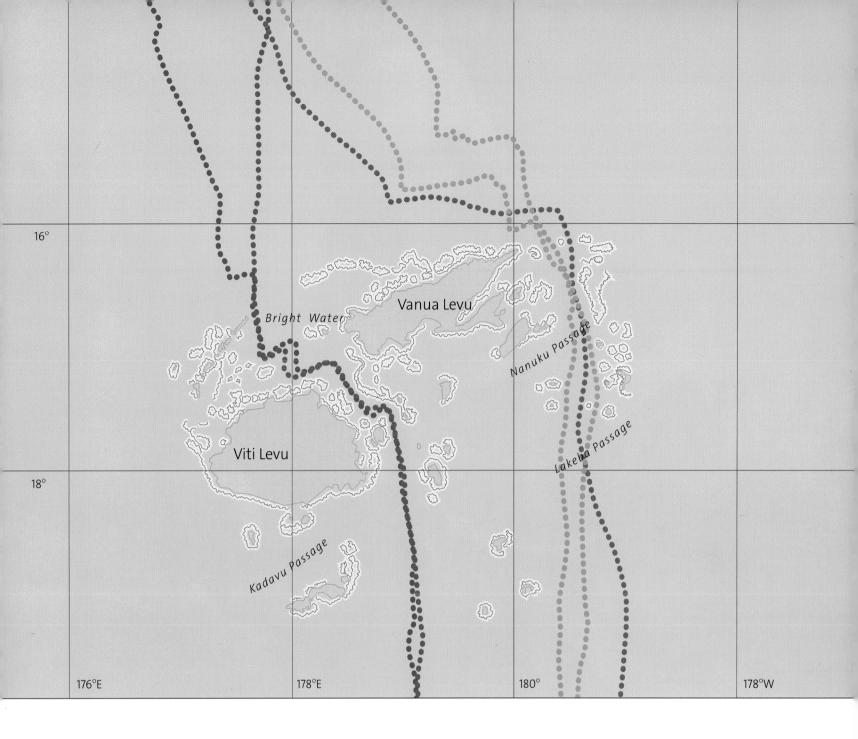

Viti Levu

Vanua Levu

Bright Water

Nanuku Passage

Lakeba Passage

Kadavu Passage

16°

18°

176°E

178°E

180°

178°W

grandfather's tugboat at the age of two. At 14, Kirby was hanging around outside the Intrepid America's Cup camp, begging for work. The crew showed him the rigging container and told him to clean it out while they went sailing. By the time Intrepid returned to the dock, the container had been emptied, swept, painted, sorted and restacked. Kirby had his foot in the door, and three weeks later he was sailing. It was the summer of 1970, the year the Beatles broke up, the year Jimi Hendrix died.

Despite all that experience, Kirby knew exactly where he stood in the decision-making process: "The eight sled dogs are on deck, blinders on, pulling the sled ... So what, you're going to go and argue with them [skipper and navigator]? Forget it; whatever they come up with, we go that way, you don't even think twice ..."

Kirby's sled-dog metaphor was bleak, if apt. They were on deck for four hours, burning every calorie they could eat and crawling into the bunk at the end of it, with little mental stimulus and virtually no knowledge of the outside world. But sceptical bells rang over something that Kirby had said earlier in Cape Town — was the atmosphere really so intense on deck that there was little or no conversation even from Jerry Kirby? It was no surprise when PUMA's media crewman, Rick Deppe, blew this image apart after Kirby returned for leg five, writing from the boat:

"I think that in one 15-minute period there he [Kirby] *took the banter from a discussion about whether or not to shake a reef out, to an extended history lesson on the carriage houses of New England and the relative merits of red cedar over slate as a roofing material, then on to a self-diagnosis of his ribs, which he thinks might be broken, and finally for this 15-minute window of time, a great story about dirt biking on the Baja peninsula with a retired line-backer who owns a bar in Tijuana."*

Kirby had been carrying the broken ribs from an incident that occured a couple of days after leaving China. It hadn't slowed him up.

The banter was not restricted to one boat either. Green Dragon's skipper Ian Walker often displayed his sense of humour in his emails. So it was no surprise when Rick Deppe reported the receipt of one that Walker had sent to Andrew Cape shortly after PUMA bore away to take on the transit of Fiji. It read, *"Nice one Capey, but are you sure you can get under the new road bridge?"* As Deppe pointed out:

"Now obviously this was a joke, the two islands are about 15 miles apart, and a bridge that size would be a pretty sizable public works programme for a small South Pacific island state which, as I understand it, has been going through some major political upheaval over the last few decades. So after one last check of ALL the charts ... we carried on."

When PUMA sailed out of the Makogai Channel and into open water south of Fiji, they had the lead. Telefónica Blue followed just over two hours later in third place, which was a remarkable comeback for a boat that had started 19 hours late. Bouwe Bekking was particularly pleased with their speed and the new rudders that they had changed to in Qingdao. He related from the boat that they were satisfied that the three-point penalty had been worth taking.

Ericsson 4 slotted into second place, with Ericsson 3 fourth and Green Dragon fifth. But Ian Walker and his team could be very happy with that. Way back on the morning of 16 February, when she had first taken a more

left PUMA's bowman Jerry Kirby (top) was on his third race around the world, seen here working at one of the more mundane tasks, using the pedestal to grind the mainsail winch. But Kirby is wearing all the kit for the more exposed parts of his job (bottom): lifejacket, safety harness and full foul-weather clothing.

easterly track than the rest, they were 40 miles behind Ericsson 4. On Saturday morning, 28 February, they were once again reaching along in the wake of Ericsson 4, and were 40 miles behind. Given that Walker had already acknowledged his boat's speed issues in these conditions, that was a result.

It looked grim for Jules Salter and the crew on Ericsson 4, but the 'Fiji-move' was far from done. The problem for PUMA and Telefónica Blue was that they were now 100 miles to the west of their main opposition, and the east was forecast to have better wind. And so it turned out. As the leverage slowly unwound, it was in Ericsson 4's favour. Forty-eight hours after the split opened, it was an extraordinarily similar picture to before all the action kicked off. Ken Read captured it when he wrote from the boat, *"When it is all said and done, I really don't think that Fiji will have been the deciding factor in this race."*

The points at the scoring gate were about to be decided, and attention quickly turned to who could get to 36 deg S first. There was one more belt of light wind and clouds to be negotiated, and Ericsson 4 finally gave up her long-held position to the east to clear it. It was a close-run thing. PUMA and Ericsson 3 got right beside them, but they couldn't quite make the pass. Once again, Salter, Grael and the rest of the team found a little extra something when it most counted, and pulled into a freshening breeze first. By the time they reached the scoring gate they were howling along in excess of 20 knots in brutal conditions, holding a 32-minute advantage over Ericsson 3, who was just 10 minutes ahead of PUMA. Telefónica Blue followed a couple of hours later, beating Green Dragon for fourth.

While all the attention had been on the sound and fury of the drag race to the scoring gate, the navigators had remained busy. History dictated a simple strategy at this point. The first boat into the Southern Ocean to meet the strong westerly winds blowing above an eastbound low-pressure system was usually the first boat to Cape Horn. But conditions were offering an alternative option, a northern route that would go above the centre of a large area of high pressure (and the light winds associated with that weather feature) forming to block the road south. Everyone had been watching the situation develop over a period of days, but history bore heavily on the shoulders of navigators and skippers who had seen such options evaporate before.

It bore a little less heavily on the youthful shoulders of Aksel Magdahl, the 29-year old navigator of Ericsson 3. Before the start in Alicante in October, the furthest distance that he had raced a sailboat was a few hundred miles. And until he started sailing professionally in 2004, he had never been a navigator. Growing up on the island of Nøtterøy in southern Norway, he had begun sailing dinghies with his family at a young age, before losing interest in favour of football and computers.

He returned to the sport in his late teens, on yachts, and this time moved up through the ranks fast. Then, after three years of racing on a professional circuit for 60-foot multihulls, he turned away from the sport again, to go back to college to complete an already much-postponed master's course in business and economics. The postgraduate degree was almost complete when he came to the attention of the Ericsson team. They were very persuasive, and the offer was a

The barrage of
instrument displays on the
back of the mast is
programmable, allowing
almost any performance or
navigation number to be
shown. While every boat will
have the displays, the
numbers that the crew
chooses to put on them will
vary both with personal taste
and the sailing conditions. In
this case it is, from top to
bottom: boat speed, true wind
angle, apparent wind angle,
heading and true wind speed.
The white tube is a static
video camera used by the
media crew and operated
from down below.

unique opportunity. So Magdahl put off his final exam,
declined a job with PricewaterhouseCoopers, and in July
2007 he joined the Nordic crew on Ericsson 3. But on
arrival at the team's training base in Lanzarote, he went
straight back into the classroom with Chris Bedford to
get a solid foundation in race meteorology.

The option that Magdahl and others were looking at
was a route that went north of the centre of the blocking
high pressure, to meet up with a newly developing low-
pressure system to the northeast. Initially, when Magdahl
first spotted it, the choice didn't look favourable. He played
it down when he briefed the crew, 24 hours out from the
scoring gate. Then, as successive weather forecasts
came in, it started to look more and more realistic.

There were many factors at work in Magdahl's
choice, but one thing was clear: it was his choice alone.
Unlike the rest of the skippers in the fleet, Ericsson 3's
Magnus Olsson spent no time working with his
navigator on strategy. Olsson was an irrepressible
60-year-old, six-time race veteran and previous race
winner. He had been a watch captain for the first three
legs, and then had temporarily replaced skipper and
fellow Swede Anders Lewander when he had been forced
to undergo knee surgery during leg four. Olsson then
got the job permanently during the Qingdao stopover.

Once in charge, Olsson elected to lead the way he
knew best – old school if you like – sailing on deck as a
watch captain, rather than following the modern style
of sharing the strategic burden down below with the
navigator. So while Olsson retained a veto on any
decision or proposition that Magdahl came up with, he
wasn't a party to the calculations or analysis. And with
horrendous conditions during the final dash to the

top   All hands to the pumps. For straight-line sailing, just four crew are on deck, while the others rest below. But sail changes normally require the full complement, and for this manoeuvre all the winch pedestals are in use, or 'loaded' as the jargon has it.

bottom   Andrew McLean (left) and Neal McDonald (right), dressed in survival suits and looking a little anxious and tired aboard Green Dragon. Sailing the boat at speeds peaking well over 30 knots in harsh conditions takes its toll on everyone on board.

scoring gate, Magdahl and Olsson had had the absolute minimum amount of time to discuss the situation, with little opportunity for the latter to develop a firm enough opinion to issue such a veto. As for the rest of the crew, as Jerry Kirby pointed out, sled dogs pulled the sled, they didn't try to guide it. If the Jerry Kirbys of this world were going to let the brains trust get on with it, the young team aboard Ericsson 3 was even less likely to interfere.

Afterwards, Magdahl was adamant that he had made a rational, numbers-based decision, using the same computerised mathematical algorithm and virtual Volvo Open 70 that Bedford used for the ensemble modelling prior to the start. The probable gains on the northern route made the choice self-evident. The weather forecast was relatively stable and, most importantly, it only had to be accurate for the next three days. He wasn't relying on the forecast still being right in a week's time for his plan to work. Nevertheless, as anyone who has left the house in the morning in a shirt and needed an overcoat by lunchtime knows, weather forecasts can be wrong over any time scale.

Of course, there was the history – all those Southern Ocean legs that had been won by boats going south. And all those people who had tried something different had failed ignominiously – a few of whom were taking part in this very race. Go south in the Southern Ocean was as old a maxim as leg one's urging to go west in the Doldrums. But the game had subtly changed with the Race Office requirement to come back northwards at two points between New Zealand and Cape Horn (known as ice gates), to keep the fleet away from drifting ice. The final factor was the Volvo Open 70 – a much quicker and more powerful boat than its

predecessors. It didn't need a 40-knot storm to hit top speeds; 25 knots of wind was plenty.

At least, that was Magdahl's argument afterwards. But he also acknowledged that other, more imponderable factors might have been at work – not finishing leg four with the rest of the fleet, for instance. The accumulation of misfortune made it certain they would not do themselves justice in the final overall standings. Perhaps everything that had gone before loosened the constraints of tactical thinking. Perhaps there was a willingness to go for the big move because to win the leg now, after all they had been through, would write an incredible story. Perhaps fate owed them that ending. Perhaps they almost had an obligation to take the chance, to go for the win. Perhaps it was the only just reward for the shore crew that had endured such back-breaking labour to get them out there.

Whatever the path to the decision, once Ericsson 3 sailed through the gate and collected the points for second, they came on to the wind and tacked to go back northeast, while everyone else sailed on to the south. The move surprised even those who had been watching the weather carefully. And for those who hadn't, there were different types of stunned reaction. Martin Krite's mother phoned Martin's wife in tears, convinced that something bad had happened to her son – why else would they be taking the strange course that was suddenly visible on the race website?

Aboard Ericsson 4, Jules Salter had been watching the formation of the low pressure since Fiji. They had been east of their major rivals – PUMA and Telefónica Blue – for almost the entire leg, precisely because they

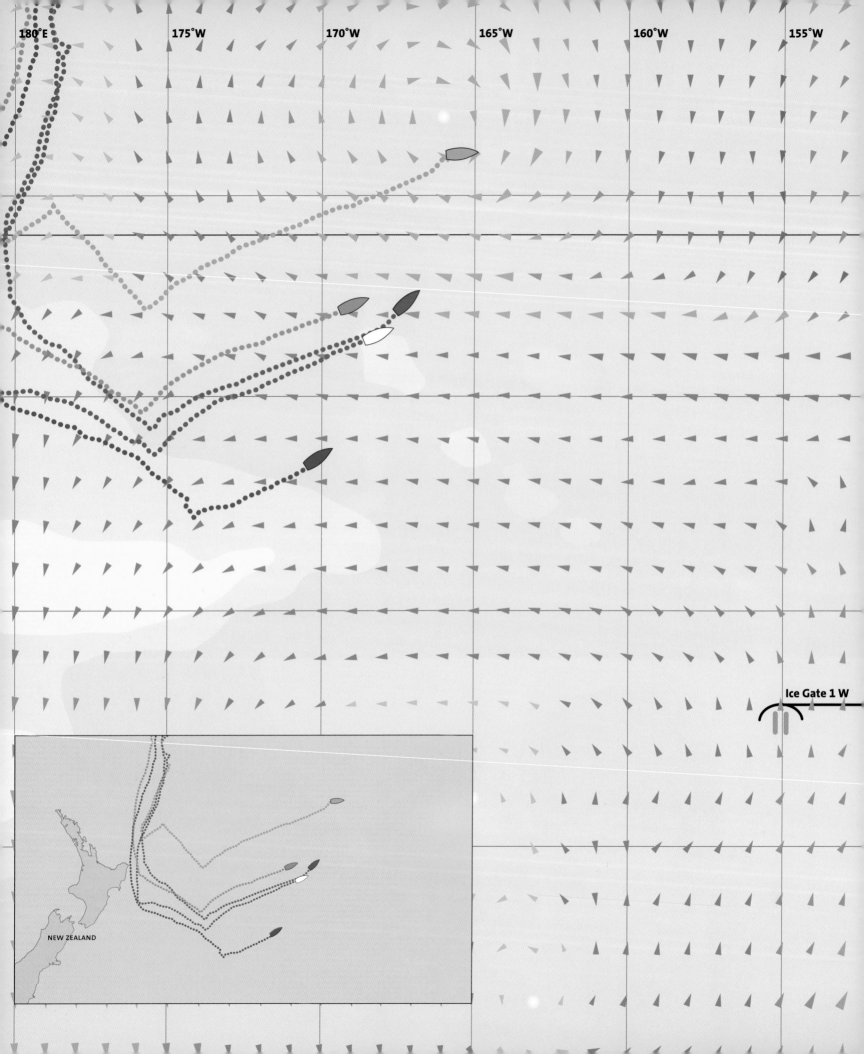

180°E 175°W 170°W 165°W 160°W 155°W

Ice Gate 1 W

NEW ZEALAND

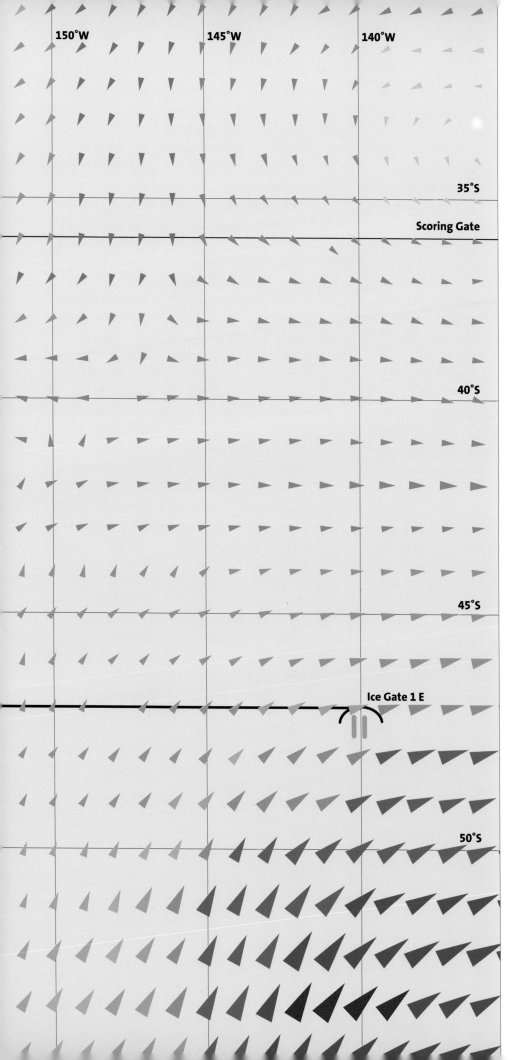

150°W 145°W 140°W

35°S

Scoring Gate

40°S

45°S

Ice Gate 1 E

50°S

were wary of the formation of such a system, and wanted to be closest to it. But now that it had formed, Salter felt the models were inconclusive as to whether it was faster than the traditional route to the south. Even more pertinent to Salter's strategic thinking was that while PUMA appeared to have decided to go north of the high-pressure centre, they weren't targeting the low. They had just turned on to the wind and headed southeast. And in an email Telefónica Blue's skipper Bouwe Bekking said, *"If that route will win them* [Ericsson 3] *the leg, they will write history, as up to now in all the legs down south, the south has won."* And he was backing that thinking with his boat positioning.

By then the separation, the north-to-south leverage across the fleet, was growing rapidly. Someone was going to get hurt. Aksel Magdahl wrote from the boat: *"I thought there was a good chance they would follow the same strategy. In most cases in this race the navigators on the leading boats have made similar choices, particularly where there could be big splits."* But this time they hadn't, and suddenly, for the young navigator aboard Ericsson 3, this had become a career-defining move. Race watchers held their breath, as though a Mayday had been issued from the Southern Ocean.

Unable to stay with PUMA and Telefónica Blue, Salter anxiously waited for the next weather forecast to see if it would resolve the dilemma. And at 12.00 GMT, it was clear that the route south was becoming less and less viable, as the high pressure slipped that way. Shortly afterwards, Ericsson 4 turned up on to the wind and started heading east – closing down the leverage as fast as they could to PUMA and Ericsson 3 to their north. Green Dragon made their eastwards turn at exactly the

left The chart tracks Ericsson 3's (orange) spectacular move to the northeast after the scoring gate off New Zealand – visible when the orange line first diverges from the others. Ericsson 3 maintained that northerly position until the moment pictured (6 March, 16.00 GMT), when they hit the centre of the low pressure that navigator Aksel Magdahl had

been targeting. Now they would turn southeast and power down in front of PUMA (red), Ericsson 4 (grey), Green Dragon (green) and Telefónica Blue (blue), all of whom were battling headwinds from the huge high pressure centred to their south. The big storm in the bottom right corner of the chart is moving away from the fleet.

same time. Despite their willingness to accept the risk of separation, they hadn't quite had the nerve for Magdahl's move, although afterwards skipper Ian Walker admitted, "We actually nearly broke away at Fiji, three or four days before Ericsson 3 did …" That left Telefónica Blue. And finally, after one more iteration of the weather forecast cycle, Bekking and Addis joined the trek across the northern side of the high pressure.

Telefónica Blue had pushed hardest to the southeast, and then, on the evening of 5 March, her forestay broke. Quick thinking on the wheel by Jonathan Swain saved the mast. The failure meant that they could only use small headsails upwind and reaching, in light and moderate wind – a desperate handicap in the predominant conditions. Worse, it forced them the wrong way for two precious hours, pushing them further into the light winds of the high pressure. Jordi Calafat told himself that it could have been worse, that they could have been facing a 20-day delivery trip to Rio without a mast, missing the in-port and perhaps even the start of leg six. "What can you do? Look at the miles, and there's 6,000 to go," he said afterwards.

Telefónica Blue sailed on, but it was another crushing setback after they had fought so hard and so successfully to get into the race again, after the grounding in Qingdao. In a telling piece of film shot on board by Gabriele Olivo, the Italian media crew, Jonathan Swain looked shattered. Afterwards, when asked if he thought they still had a chance of the overall win, he said, "If you want to be a realist it's going to be flipping hard; if you want to be a dreamer then you can keep telling yourself, OK, we still have

half the points to race for." Telefónica Blue's crew stabilised the rig as well as they could, and joined the others on a northeasterly course. By then, there was over 450 miles of north-to-south separation between Telefónica Blue and Ericsson 3 – and Magdahl's plan was unfolding just as he had hoped.

The Nordic team battled their way upwind towards the centre of the low pressure in rough, confused seas. It was tough, potentially boat-breaking sailing. The strategy was always going to mean a physical risk, as well as a tactical one. And Magdahl was well aware of his lack of experience in making those kinds of judgements. But they came through it and, according to Martin Krite, it was nothing like as bad as the conditions they had suffered on leg four. They escaped into the light and variable breeze in the centre of the low on the afternoon of 6 March, and soon after into the strong northerly wind on the other side. Immediately they tacked to port, and started to scream back to the southeast.

By the morning of 7 March, it was clear that Ericsson 3 had pulled off a brilliant coup. As she blasted down to a position east of PUMA, Green Dragon and Ericsson 4 – getting almost directly between them and Cape Horn – she was over 100 miles ahead. It was one of the most remarkable moves the race had seen for a long while and Magdahl was rightly applauded. Not that the man himself wasn't pleased, writing from the boat as he celebrated his 30th birthday:

"It will be an unforgettable birthday, really, sailing straight into the middle of the low pressure with bad sea state and variable breeze, trying to nail a big lead on THE leg of this Volvo Ocean Race. Stopping dead becalmed in the centre of the low, then screaming out on the other side … and gaining …"

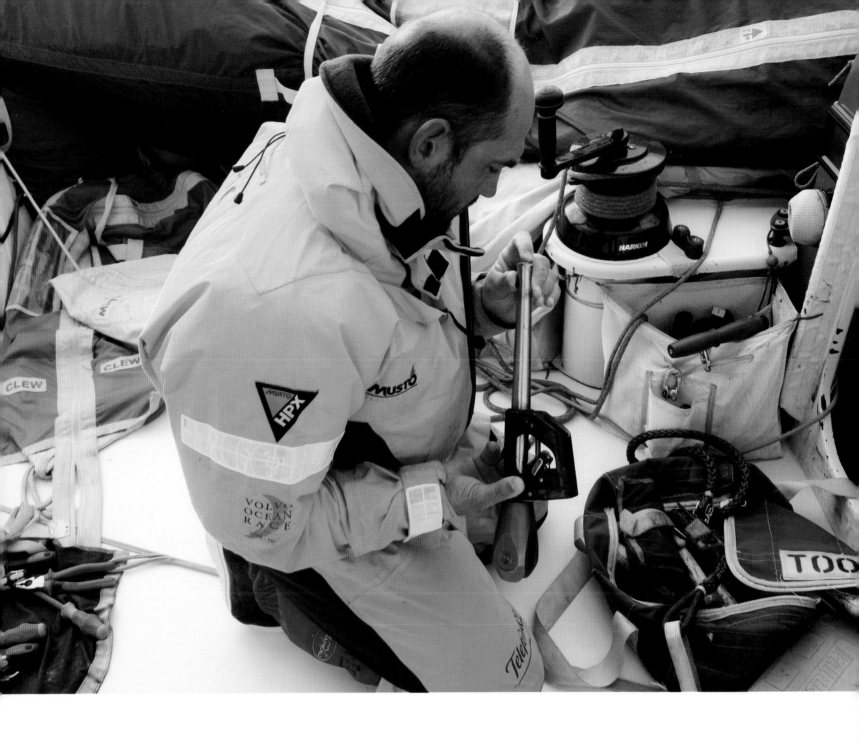

Aboard PUMA, Ken Read and Andrew Cape had talked through the option Ericsson 3 had taken with their watch captains. No one had wanted to take the chance – it wasn't just a question of the tactical risk, but there was also residual anxiety about putting the boat through the rough seas of the low, after the issues they had on legs one and four. As Jerry Kirby said afterwards, "Knowing the history of our boat, if we got into 45 knots, on the wind, we'd probably break it. So that's Ericsson 3 – where do we stand with them; OK, they're going north, hmmm, everybody else is going this way ... There're two things: asset preservation and point positioning." And for PUMA, both of them said let Ericsson 3 go – she wasn't a threat overall, and the guys that were a threat were to the south.

But by then, unknown to his team-mates, Jerry Kirby was finding it hard to worry about the intricacies of the yacht race too much any more. His wife, Kim, had been diagnosed with skin cancer just after the leg had started, but she had only finally told him via email when the boat was through the scoring gate and off New Zealand. By then, she was into a process of three operations that she would have before Kirby could get back to her side:
"Talk about feeling helpless, you should be home ... suddenly the game changed, like 42 days I was prepared – I can take anything ... But nothing in my sailing career has ever been like that, you're like ... holy s***, I gotta get home ... and I'm off New Zealand, and you've got the Southern Ocean ahead. Getting up for every watch and staying focused, 'cause it's such a dangerous boat and we're going into more dangerous s*** and I'm trying to support my wife with emails ... it was a really interesting time, interesting leg. She's just ... I got more

admiration for her, I told her, you are way tougher than any of the guys on this boat, she's held it all together."

While Kirby suffered on PUMA, Jules Salter was working hard on a strategy for Ericsson 4's recovery. Now having decided to go for the low pressure, they committed to it completely. PUMA was a little more tentative, and by 8 March, Ericsson 4 was into second place. Speeds picked up significantly once they were all in the strong northerly breeze on the other side and they charged towards the second ice gate. But it quickly became clear that the weather system was pulling ahead of the yachts as it moved east. Behind the leading three, Green Dragon made an aggressive move to the south to hold the breeze, while PUMA and Ericsson 4 were both forced to watch the leader build her advantage to 300 miles as she held on to the system and clocked up one 500-mile day after another.

Green Dragon's move had taken them all the way to 50 deg S, and on 11 March, Ian Walker reported: *"It's 02.30 local time and I am just boiling some water for hot drinks. 'Ian, is the radar on? We can see some objects in the water.' These were the exact words of Animal [Andrew McLean], being a typically understated Kiwi – anybody else would have run down the hatch shouting 'iceberg 2 o'clock' or something else out of the Titanic ... The three that we saw in rapid succession were each between 100 metres across and the size of a football pitch as best we could tell in the dark about a half a mile away ... I noticed this morning that a few more people are now wearing survival suits and we have made a point of closing all the water tight doors."*

Green Dragon's sighting of icebergs was a part of the Southern Ocean experience that most were happy

left　Fast sailing on PUMA, but the relentless round of equipment checks can't be stopped because of the torrid conditions. So someone just has to go up there and get wet.

to miss. So far, the ice gates had largely done their job of keeping the boats north and away from the worst of the conditions. Now, with the leader clearing the second ice gate, there was no man-made obstacle between her and Cape Horn at 57 deg S. But as Ericsson 3 turned her bow southwards, the challenge she confronted was not ice, monster waves or shrieking winds; it was calms. Yet another area of high pressure started to form across a contrary Southern Ocean to block the route to Cape Horn.

By the time Ericsson 4 and PUMA arrived at the ice gate half a day later, they had significantly closed the gap. They set off southeast in pursuit of Ericsson 3, but already another low-pressure system was forming to the northeast in an eerily familiar pattern. And by the time Green Dragon arrived at the ice gate on 13 March, she ignored the opportunity to turn south towards the Horn and instead continued east, to intercept the low pressure and ride south with it.

One by one the skippers and navigators of the leading trio acknowledged that riding the low pressure represented the fastest way for all of them to reach Cape Horn, as the area of high pressure and light wind solidified in front of them. Everyone diverted their course eastwards. The last to do so was the leader, Ericsson 3. It took a while for Aksel Magdahl to become resigned to the fact that the low would sweep south, pick them up one at a time, and push the top four back together. But it was a similar weather pattern to the way Ericsson 3 had caught up so quickly out of Qingdao, as well as being similar to the low they had ridden into the lead after the scoring gate. Live by the sword, die by the sword.

The low-pressure system finally brought with it the Southern Ocean conditions that everyone expected – just in time for Green Dragon engineer Tom Braidwood to have his birthday. It was some present. As Torben Grael wrote from Ericsson 4, *"The rookies must have been wondering if all those stories about it were true. But now, with 1,000 miles to go it looks like we are all going to have a good taste of it."*

Aboard Ericsson 3, Swedish media crew Gustav Morin had earlier asked one of those rookies about his attitude to the risks of sailing, given his calling to the priesthood. And Martin Krite replied, "I think for me, my belief is helping me a lot every day in different situations, and also when I'm sailing out here; but it's not as though I go up and do crazy things in the rig or on the bow because I think that something good will happen if I fall off. It doesn't work like that." Each boat wrestled with its demons as the weather and the world closed in around them. From Green Dragon, Ian Walker wrote, *"There is noticeably less chat amongst the guys as everyone is in survival mode just personally trying to get through the next few days."*

Ericsson 4's New Zealand boat captain David Endean was often woken by a sudden motion or noise, a change in rhythm that indicated trouble. They had already had one close call. Endean was thrown around in his bunk as the boat veered wildly from rail-to-rail, near-gybe to near-broach, as the men on deck fought to control her at 36 knots in a 60-knot squall with a broken steering sheave – a replica of the failure Green Dragon had suffered on leg two. But this one was caught on film by the static aft camera, and even Endean admitted to

left Jonathan Swain views a
cold, harsh world from behind
the protection of his visor. He
is also wearing a survival suit,
made from waterproof
(usually breathable) material.
The suits use waterproof zips,
with wrist and neck seals
made from soft latex rubber,
or built-in latex socks, to keep
the wearer as dry and warm
as possible.

feeling a little uneasy when he saw how close they had come to a major crash.

On this occasion, however, there was no follow-up shout of "Everyone up", from on deck. Endean glanced at the watch strapped above the bunk, and had a sudden rush of panic – quarter to the hour. Only 15 minutes until he was due up on deck, and he needed at least 30 minutes to check the boat and get ready. He struggled out of his sleeping bag and fished amongst the clothing distributed around the bunk. He needed to get his waterproof, breathable socks on before he did anything else; everything inside the boat was damp, and nothing – nothing – was more important than keeping his feet dry.

He got his feet into his boots, and stumbled to the toilet. There could be a queue for this facility on occasions, but no one else seemed to be stirring, so he had a free run at it. The toilet roll had been left up against the wall of the cubicle, and was sodden with condensation and completely useless. Grim, but not unusual, so Endean got on with it as best he could. As Green Dragon's New Zealand rookie Chris Main had written earlier in the leg, *"For those keen to get some Volvo experience, you could try using the loo in a caravan while being towed around a motocross track at 100 km/hr."*

Endean returned to his bunk to finish getting dressed. He had slept in some of his clothes – they had more chance of drying on the body than anywhere else, thanks to the remorseless condensation. Now he struggled into his thermal shirt and trousers, bracing himself against the boat's movement. A second set with a wind-proofing layer followed. He called to Joca Signorini, his Brazilian watch partner, also not yet up. They

were really late now, and Endean still had to check the boat before he went on deck. When Signorini appeared, wearing just his thermals, he looked confused. "Are we doing a sail change?" he asked, peering about him. That would require the whole crew, but no one else was up. They were late on deck, Endean told him. Signorini glanced at his watch and shook his head. There was an hour to go, he insisted.

The watch on Endean's bunk belonged to fellow Kiwi Tony Mutter, and was set to New Zealand time. It was 13 hours ahead of the boat – enough to fool Endean's quick, sleepy glance into thinking he was late. And now he was almost fully dressed, and an hour early. He didn't know whether to be happy or horrified – there was no point in trying to go back to sleep. It would take him 15 minutes to undress, another 15 to dress again, and by the time he'd checked the boat, he'd have about 10 minutes in bed. So he put the kettle on, made coffee, took his time with the checks, and then went on deck a little early, to the amusement of everyone else on board. But the crews needed to find things to smile at: life was basic at the best of times, but in the Southern Ocean it was elemental.

It was standard practice to issue each crew member with a small bag that they were allowed to take on board. If it didn't fit in the bag, it didn't go on the boat. Inside, there would be a toothbrush and almost certainly an iPod – the relaxation tool of choice for the 21st-century round-the-world racer. And that was it, apart from clothing, and the only clothing duplicated would be the layers worn closest to the body. In cold weather that was a two-piece thermal base layer. In hot

left   Ericsson 4 comes desperately close to a serious crash as the steering fails at 36 knots of boat speed in a 60-knot squall. The sequence runs from top left to bottom right, and was captured by the static video camera positioned at the stern of the boat.

weather it was a sun-proof, long-sleeved shirt designed to 'wick' sweat away from the skin. For the potential 40 days of leg five, Endean took just three sets of the former and two of the latter, so they were all worn for at least a week before being discarded.

Everything had to be carefully managed, otherwise chaos ensued. If any clothing came on or off it needed to go back in the bag. If the stack of gear was moved while you were on deck and something was loose, it might not reappear until the end of the leg – if at all. And even when you were being careful, it could take 15 minutes just to find your bag at the end of a watch, when all you wanted to do was get your head down.

One thing that had improved from previous races was that both boots and shoes were now allowed on board. So no one had to choose one or the other. On a leg that encompassed the northern hemisphere winter, the tropics and the Southern Ocean, that would have been an impossible decision.

There was not enough diesel fuel on the boat to generate water for anything other than drinking and rehydrating food. A rain shower in the tropics provided the only opportunity to wash either oneself or any clothes. Otherwise it was a splash on the face if you were lucky and a baby wipe or two. It didn't come close to getting off the ingrained layers of sunblock and salt. As New Zealand watch captain Stu Bannatyne later commented, "I'm lucky I don't have sensitive skin or anything, so I just pretty much don't wash or clean and I'm fine. I can go a 40-day leg without washing, no problem."

Apart from the contents of their single bag, everything else – gas for the cooker, toilet roll, toothpaste and razors – was packed in the food bags,

each containing supplies for two or three days. Unsurprisingly, 90 per cent of the time all of this stuff ran out before the end of its allotted period. Nevertheless, in theory, Endean and his team-mates regarded hygiene as critical – sickness of any kind could sweep through the boat and seriously hinder performance. It didn't stop Ericsson 4's media crew, Guy Salter (Jules's younger brother) from reporting, *"Two individuals ... have revealed that they can count on one hand the amount of times they have cleaned their teeth ..."* No one was blaming the lack of toothpaste.

As everyone expected, Ericsson 3 saw her lead slashed, piling the pressure on as they faced some of the toughest sailing conditions of the race. If there was a moment when Olsson's young crew was going to crack this was it, and the seasoned veterans behind them knew it. They all pushed as hard as they dared, but Ericsson 4's steering-gear problem and another broken wheel on PUMA helped to give the Nordics the breathing space they needed. Ericsson 3 led through the second scoring gate and around Cape Horn on 17 March. It was blowing 30 knots and, while it was rough, conditions were no longer out of control.

Ericsson 4 followed them through just two and a half hours later, with PUMA third that evening. Green Dragon didn't quite make it round on the Irish National Day – it was 02.15 on the morning of 18 March when they passed into the Atlantic. Since most people were still celebrating St Paddy's Day at that stage, no one noticed, and it counted all the same. A day and a half later, Telefónica Blue joined them in the South Atlantic. Everyone paid their proper respects to the landmark,

cigars were smoked, and secret liquor stashes were broken open. Aboard PUMA, Casey Smith got naked as promised, and even skipper Ken Read – who had been posing as something of a Horn-refusenik – finally got it: *"I just wanted to tick the box, but now I'm a believer in the power of Cape Horn."*

Ericsson 4 got within six miles of Ericsson 3 just north of the Le Maire Strait, as they both sat becalmed in the wind shadow of Tierra del Fuego. It wasn't quite close enough. Salter and his team-mates had to watch as the Nordics escaped into the breeze first and quickly rebuilt their lead to 50 miles. There were still 2,000 miles to go, and the fleet was made to suffer through fickle conditions for almost every one of them. But the 'squeeze box' was at work – the gaps between the boats compressing and opening periodically, without any real passing lanes.

Green Dragon had a particularly dreadful hand dealt to them, as the wind shifted so that they had to tack round the northern tip of the Falkland Islands. Unfortunately, those extra hours were costly, as they then didn't quite make it across in front of a growing chasm of light air. PUMA slipped through, and a huge gap started to open between the Dragon and the leading trio. It was so calm for them on the final run up to Rio that on two consecutive nights, watch captain Neal McDonald could see the stars reflected in the ocean – something he had never experienced before in hundreds of thousands of ocean-racing miles.

The slow pace brought the topic of food, a simmering issue for a while, to the fore. It was a surprise to anyone who had heard Ericsson 4's Stu Bannatyne declare,

before the start in Alicante, that food shortages were a thing of the past. In theory, the freedom to move all the gear around the boat (the rule had been removed) had made it unnecessary to skimp on the weight of something as important as food (or boots and shoes).

Standard rations on all the boats were substantial; every day the crew could expect two or three main freeze-dried meals. Each of these was usually prepared in a big, insulated pot, as the food might sit for a couple of hours before everyone had a chance to eat. Two kettles of boiling water were added to the meal packet, stirred together and left for 30 minutes. If it wasn't stirred properly, the last to arrive would get inedible, cold, crunchy powder from the bottom of the pot. These meals were supplemented with snacks – perhaps chocolate or muesli bars, shared bags of dried fruit, and two-minute noodles and soup. It added up to around 6,000 calories a person. And it was fortunate that the daily rations were so substantial, because despite the planned good intentions, by the end almost all the boats were running out.

"We started with 40 days [food supply] *and a week ago we split some food packs down to make another two days of food rations. This would give us 42 or another three days from now. We may well need at least seven days and three into seven doesn't go ... We are already hungry and it will get worse – simple as that. That is life – nobody is going to die."* So Ian Walker reported from Green Dragon, and shortly afterwards, he decided that the food would be split between each of the two-man watches, so everyone was responsible for their own supply.

Tom Braidwood was filmed helping to sort it out, and suggesting that they added strips of toilet paper to

left **In some of the seas and oceans that they sailed through, the boats were often accompanied by wildlife, as seen here with Green Dragon. But several crews commented on the apparent absence of life in the Indian Ocean, an area that the race was visiting for the first time.**

the soup to bulk it up. No one was sure if he was joking – particularly after he swallowed some to prove it was edible. Neal McDonald was sharing with his watch partner, the Irish bowman Justin Slattery. The different rationing strategies employed caused some entertainment as the days dragged on – the crew dividing into gorgers and hoarders. McDonald and Slattery set aside one cooked meal out of the normal two for the last couple of days, which put them into the hoarding camp. It could have been a lot worse, reckoned McDonald afterwards. In the 2001–02 race, they had gone to half rations just two weeks into leg one.

Aboard PUMA, Rick Deppe was in charge of the catering, as were many of the other media crew on their own boats. PUMA had also provisioned for 40 days. But as the leg stretched out in the light winds to an indeterminate finish time, there was much discussion about how to manage the last few days of food. Deppe was in favour of not rationing at all until the two boats ahead of them had finished. That would optimise their performance on the run in, until they were effectively no longer racing, as Green Dragon was hundreds of miles behind.

And so that's how they did it. The final meal was at 22.00 GMT on 26 March, and they finished at 04.27 GMT on 27 March with not a single edible scrap on the boat. For the last three days, Deppe had measured portion sizes in a mug to ensure that there were no arguments, and while he caught plenty of flak, it remained good natured. But he was fortunate that they were so close to the finish for the final meal.

Deppe had been saving all the spare spice packets for several days, to combine them into a "mystery mash"

extravaganza with the final pack of freeze-dried mashed potato. There was no shortage of anticipation when Deppe went below to prepare this last supper. But as he opened the packet there was a telltale puff of powder and a smell that was definitely not potato. It was chocolate, hot chocolate – and Deppe then had to return on deck to confess. The news wasn't well received, and he was relieved that they finished six hours later, and not six days.

If there was an explanation for the rather marginal quantities of food carried it was not so much in the weight as the sheer volume of it, which had to be accommodated along with all the other stuff required for 40 days at sea. There just wasn't enough room – the bunks wouldn't even lower properly on PUMA when they left Qingdao. But McDonald had another explanation:

"Nobody wants to be at sea for six weeks, we all know the predictions are for 42 days, 41 days, but you're saying that's the outside. It's part of human nature to be saying … we can't be at sea for any longer than that. For some it was just denial, nobody wanted to be out there for that long …"

It did end eventually though – everything does – and it did so with the most extraordinary triumph for Magnus Olsson and his Nordic crew aboard Ericsson 3. They came back from a seven-hour deficit at the start line to complete the leg in a little over 40 days, winning by 12 hours from their sister ship, Ericsson 4. They had claimed the lead with a spectacular tactical move, but to hold on to it through a torrid mix of Southern Ocean lows and Atlantic highs had taken the real grit and coolness.

A calm, professional approach had dominated from the start. They forgot nothing in the 55-minute pit stop in Qingdao, while PUMA, who had all week to pack and prepare, managed to leave behind the bulk of the sunblock. So it was a frazzled and hungry PUMA crew that finally finished third, with Green Dragon gathering valuable points in fourth. A disappointed Bouwe Bekking and his Telefónica Blue team did at least keep their rig upright all the way into Rio, which won the Wallenius Wilhelmsen Logistics Seamanship Award for Spanish bowman David Vera.

Gaunt and unshaven men stepped ashore in Rio, and in answer to the question, "So, 40 or more days at sea, 11 guys, not much space, short of food ... how did you all get on?" they answered to a man, "You have your moments, but you get over it." No one, it seemed, went crazy. Or did they? Just before they finished, PUMA's Rick Deppe reported in a final email:

"If there's a shoe floating around in the bilge on its own, I could probably guess to within two people whose it is, same with an unwashed coffee mug. I know who will be first out of his bunk and up on deck to help out when he's off watch. I know who is grumpy in the morning, and who can stay up all night and keep smiling. I even know who the chocolate robber is – but I'll never tell."

The code of silence was alive and well aboard all Volvo Open 70s. If anyone had lost it, no one was talking.

After Telefónica Blue finished, skipper Bouwe Bekking requested that the point scores for the leg be adjusted, because the fault for their grounding at the start in Qingdao lay with the Race management. To no one's particular surprise, the International Jury didn't agree – it seemed that some bad things just happened.

But less than a week after they finished leg five, Telefónica Blue redeemed themselves with a sparkling win in the in-port racing in Rio, chased home by Ken Read and PUMA.

In his home waters and in front of his home crowd, Torben Grael and Ericsson 4 could only manage a fourth place, beaten by Delta Lloyd, fresh out of the repair shop off a ship from Singapore. The results undid some of the damage that Ericsson 4 had done to their pursuit in leg five, but they were still a long way ahead overall, with a 9.5-point lead over PUMA, newly installed in second place, who was a further two points clear of Telefónica Blue. If leg five was a tipping point, it had tipped in Ericsson 4's favour. They might not have won the leg, but they had pulled well clear of the chasing pack. And Jules Salter was still in his job.

left　**Victory peels back the years for Ericsson 3's veteran skipper, Magnus Olsson. If winning leg five was a valedictory moment, then it was one that everyone will remember.**

It was 77 days since Telefónica Black had withdrawn from leg four of the Volvo Ocean Race, turning back from the fury of the Kuroshio and a northeast monsoon storm to return to Singapore; 77 days of shipping, logistics and repair work, 77 days for the crew to get rusty and forget how to sail their boat. Or was it 77 days for the crew to rest and recuperate, to prepare mentally and physically for the challenge of returning to the race? As the gun went on 11 April 2009 it certainly appeared to be the latter.

Rio de Janeiro had turned on all her sultry charm. Under a glorious blue sky, in a light southwesterly sea breeze, Telefónica Black won the start and sailed into a lead as clear as the sunshine. She controlled the fleet to the windward mark and led smoothly around the second lap, but like the swan that floats, apparently serene on the surface while paddling frantically below, there was drama on board. South African bowman Mike Pammenter had stepped into a loop of slack rope just as the boat started to tack. The rope went tight and slammed his leg unmercifully into the base of the mast.

Pammenter took his beating quietly. The first that Swedish navigator and medic Roger Nilson knew about it was when, 20 minutes later, he was asked to take a look at the ankle as they turned south out of Guanabara Bay. The course took them around the base of the Pão de Açúcar to a buoy set off Copacabana Beach, and Nilson had plenty else to worry about as they led the fleet down the shore in the light conditions and a crashing swell. Pammenter's ankle was bruised and swollen with an ugly haematoma. After a careful examination, Nilson decided that there was no fracture and that the injury would heal itself. He strapped the ankle and Pammenter

limped back up to the foredeck. There was a race to win: after a poor start in front of his home crowd, Torben Grael was leading Ericsson 4 on a charge up through the fleet and closing fast.

Nilson knew that he could call on an extensive medical kit: the contents reflected the race's many years' cumulative experience dealing with whatever befell the human body on a powerful, fast-moving sailboat. The equipment included staple guns, needles and glue to stop bleeding; antibiotics to deal with infections; and splints for fractures, including equipment to stabilise the neck and immobilise a patient in a bunk in case of a spinal injury. They had everything they needed for intravenous therapy; a tracheotomy; burns treatment; and intramuscular and subcutaneous injections. Each boat had two trained medics aboard – although Nilson's advantage was that he had qualified as a doctor, even though it was almost 20 years since he had practised.

Plenty of the equipment and training had already been tested. Tony Mutter's evacuation from Ericsson 4 at the Cape Verde Islands on leg one was simply the most dramatic event. It sat alongside a steady drip of injuries – concussions, torn ligaments, prolapsed vertebrae discs, mangled fingertips, broken ribs, kettle burns, haemorrhoids and kidney infections – which had been responsible for many of the crew changes to date. Only Ericsson 4 had managed to keep the same crew through to the start of leg six. In contrast, their sister ship had made nine changes to offshore crew in the same period.

The Race management's medical coordinator, Polly Gough, was compiling some telling statistics

chapter opener Delta Lloyd and Telefónica Black rejoin the fleet; seven yachts at the dock in Rio ahead of the leg six start. But sailing on his home waters in the in-port race turned out to be no advantage for Ericsson 4's Brazilian skipper, Torben Grael. The advantage of knowing the

area can be outweighed by the added pressure and distractions of sailing in front of a home crowd.

left PUMA and Ericsson 4 chase Telefónica Black into a turning mark during the lap of Guanabara Bay, before the boats headed outside to round the Pão de Açúcar. All three are ready to hoist spinnakers; the sails are attached to the end of the bowsprit and draped back into the boat.

overleaf Telefónica Black leads Ericsson 4 and PUMA around the Pão de Açúcar, accompanied by the spectator fleet and a big swell crashing on to the rocks around the base of one of Rio's most familiar landmarks.

through the questionnaires filled in at the end of each leg. By the time Mike Pammenter cracked his ankle into the mast there had already been 349 reported medical issues from 107 sailing days, an average of one per boat every other day. While the big, bloody, concussive injuries usually grabbed the space in news reports, the most common complaint was the same one that had forced Ericsson 4's detour to the Cape Verde Islands: the fungal infections and sores on infected skin. There were 59 reported cases on the first five legs of the race – clearly not everyone could cope as well as Stu Bannatyne and go 40-plus days without washing!

Despite the distraction of the injury, Telefónica Black held her lead to the mark off Copacabana Beach. The course then took the fleet eastwards to Cabo Frio, just along the coast from Rio. The headland stood between them and the turn northwards towards the scoring gate at the island of Fernando de Noronha (which had also been a scoring gate on leg one). Then it was onwards into the North Atlantic, towards the completion of the 4,900 miles of leg six in Boston on the northeast coast of the USA.

It was just after the Copacabana mark when Telefónica Black's skipper, Fernando Echávarri, asked Roger Nilson to take a second look at Michael Pammenter's ankle. It was an hour later, and the swelling had increased. The strapping clearly wasn't making much difference. Nilson could no longer discount the possibility of a fracture, and they made the decision to get Pammenter off the boat before they got much further from Rio. The evacuation was a simple matter compared with that of Tony Mutter. Phone calls were made to the duty officer and the Telefónica shore

team, and soon a RIB (rigid inflatable boat) was powering out to meet them at the Ilhas Maricas. Pammenter stepped, very carefully, off the Volvo Open 70, and was soon back on the dockside in the Marina da Glória, giving embarrassed interviews. "I am really upset, I just feel pretty stupid to be honest. We are all really excited to leave and then I do something like this. But it happens."

The sea breeze that had powered them out of Guanabara Bay and along the coast to Copacabana died quickly as the sun set. The wind shifted back to an easterly direction and became very soft. It did not go well for Telefónica Blue. They had been duelling for third or fourth, but then Ericsson 4 just sailed away from them as the fleet headed offshore. Afterwards, Spanish helmsman Jordi Calafat thought that the problem might have been that in the darkness they had unknowingly sat in the confused and turbulent wind coming off the other boat's sails. Whatever it was, they quickly found themselves at the back of the fleet with Green Dragon.

The conditions were frustrating and uncomfortable, with just two to three knots of wind and a three-metre swell rolling in from the south. But, as Calafat saw it, if there was no wind offshore, it could hardly be any worse inshore. Why not try the beach? They were already as good as last. And theory backed the prospect of a night-time land breeze – a wind created by cooling, heavier air from a higher elevation, flowing down a slope under the force of gravity. Along with Green Dragon, they tacked and sailed back towards the shore.

It took a while to get there, two or three hours of ugly drifting, rolling over the swell with the sails

slatting: crashing against the mast and rigging. But then came a moment only too familiar to Calafat from his island home of Palma de Mallorca. He could smell the land. It was tangibly different from the salt smell all around them: cooking, a fire, maybe a barbecue. And, knowing exactly what was coming next, he called for the crew to get ready to tack. The bowman dashed forward, but the new wind hit them almost immediately, throwing the boat into what Calafat called an "auto-tack"; the boat tacked without changing course as the new wind arrived from the opposite direction to the old wind.

Suddenly they were sailing in what felt like a gale. It was only six or seven knots, but it was blowing from the north, off the land, allowing them to point directly east towards Cabo Frio. And, slowly, Calafat picked out a fixed constellation of red port bow lights against the background confusion of fishing boats and shipping. It was the rest of the Volvo Open 70s, all moving together, but dropping back. Telefónica Blue kept close to the coast to stay in the land breeze, Green Dragon in their wake. By early on the Sunday morning the pair were into the lead, still ghosting along the beach. They rounded Cabo Frio with an advantage of four to five miles over Ericsson 4 and PUMA, who were at the front of the pursuing pack.

Green Dragon's watch captain Neal McDonald had done five of these races, and reckoned days two and three of any leg were always the worst. It was the transition between shore and sea life that was hardest. On the first day the adrenaline was pumping and no one slept much anyway, and by day three the crew was getting into the new rhythm. It was the bit in-between that was tough, and on this leg it was not being made any easier by the conditions. Rick Deppe wrote from PUMA, *"My own theory is that people are still recovering from the physical and mental toll taken on them by leg five, there's been no real downtime for months now, so being out here and going between zero and three knots is understandably frustrating."*

Ericsson 4's Kiwi watch captain Stu Bannatyne wrote of his own concerns:
"In Rio, there was barely enough time to regain weight, let alone any conditioning or strength lost on the previous leg. This means that most of the sailors on leg six will still be at sub-optimum physically. Add to this the travelling for the guys that flew home from Rio and it makes for a tough turn around. Leg six will also be tough as we make many sail changes in hot weather and then at the end will likely be in freezing cold temperatures as we approach Boston."

Eventually, the southeasterly trade winds filled in across the fleet, Telefónica Blue holding her lead as they did so, and the pack settled into the chase in a tight group. These are some of the most stable winds on the planet and, with almost 3,000 miles to go through the south and northeast trade winds, the crews finally eased back into the familiar, comforting pattern of the watch system. McDonald had explained that no one now considered it efficient to change the whole watch at the same time. The old system had been to split the crew into two sets of four, with each working four hours on and four hours off. But it meant that all the knowledge of the wind conditions, the sea state and the fast set-up left the deck and went below at the same

left **Green Dragon fends off Ericsson 3 on the beaches of Rio de Janeiro. A big swell and not much wind made the start of leg six particularly unpleasant as the fleet sailed to a mark off Copacabana Beach, and then east to Cabo Frio.**

overleaf left **A spinnaker comes down on the windward side of Ericsson 3, being pulled through the main hatch by the crew below. The job of the man on deck is to try and guide it down, freeing any snags before they turn into rips.**

overleaf right **Ericsson 4 and PUMA both prepare to drop spinnakers by letting them fly loose in the wind shadow of the mainsail, so that there is less resistance to the crew pulling them down. The replacement sail is the headsail, which you can just see starting to fill at the front of Ericsson 4.**

AM WORLD PORT WORLD CITY

time. Such discontinuity was inefficient as the new watch struggled to sail the boat quickly while they familiarised themselves with the conditions.

The system had begun to change three or four races previously, with the crew now paired up into four watches of two men, with the watch changing every two hours. Continuity was now ensured by the new watch joining two men who had already been on deck for a couple of hours. It was a rhythm that, once established, the crews could maintain for days or weeks, as required. But while McDonald may have been happy with a watch system he had seen develop through his five-race career, he was a lot less happy with Green Dragon's performance as they raced for the points at the scoring gate. Second at Cabo Frio, they gradually, painfully, slipped backwards. The trade-wind sailing was straight-line reaching, boat-speed sailing – and Green Dragon was notoriously slow in those conditions.

A boat that should have been struggling was Delta Lloyd, the only boat in this race that had been built for the previous edition. Like Telefónica Black, the team had taken an enforced break while the boat was shipped to Brazil and repaired. But they had returned even more forcefully to the competition with a place on the podium in the Rio de Janeiro in-port race. And after being the first to move offshore at Cabo Frio, they had benefited as the trade winds arrived from the east. Now the winner of the earlier race was demonstrating that in some conditions she still had the pace, moving up to second as Green Dragon slipped back. However, Telefónica Blue's skipper, Bouwe Bekking, wasn't surprised to see the old boat as he looked over his

shoulder: *"When we designed this boat* [Telefónica Blue], *we did a model of the race winner from last time* [Delta Lloyd] *and it was shown to be as good as ours, not a fraction slower when tight reaching, as they have a very powerful hull."*

Dutchman Gerd-Jan Poortman was one of only four of the leg one crew still aboard Delta Lloyd for leg six. The changes didn't seem to have done them any more harm than the break from racing. The boat's late entry to the race in Alicante had left Poortman with no time for the physical conditioning that he would normally undertake for his job on the bow. But he hadn't wasted the opportunity that the break had provided. He had spent lots of tough hours in the gym doing a mix of cardio and core stability work, along with upper-body weight training. But there were limits to what physical conditioning and enthusiasm could do against the well-trained and highly practised machine that was Ericsson 4. The overall leaders finally went past about 24 hours from the scoring gate. Delta Lloyd just wasn't competitive across a wide range of conditions and, unlike Ericsson 4, they didn't have the months of sail testing and training to enable them to respond as efficiently to changes in conditions.

By 16 April, that ability was proving invaluable, as the fleet sailed into a highly unstable area of clouds just as the pressure was on for the final dash to the scoring gate. PUMA's skipper Ken Read later called it the "sail changing world championships". On the bow of Delta Lloyd, Poortman was in a tough repêchage round for third place, and grateful for all that work in the gym. It was relentless. In 16 knots of wind speed with a wind angle just past the beam, the boat rolled along happily

left **One of many sail changes aboard Delta Lloyd, as Gerd-Jan Poortman (right) and Morgan White (left) pack a headsail. Choosing the right sail to put up next in rapidly changing conditions is vital, as the transition could cost a couple of miles of distance, even when it goes smoothly.**

with the big masthead code zero flying off the bowsprit. Then the wind shifted a little, making the angle too tight for the zero. It had to be furled and lowered to the deck, 80 kilograms of unmanageable snaking sail cloth that the Telefónica Black crew had nicknamed the 'Anaconda'.

It was replaced by a barely more manageable, slightly smaller version called the fractional zero. It didn't quite reach all the way to the masthead, but it was a snip to move around at just 70 kilograms when it was dry – which it wasn't by the time they'd hauled it out of the stack of sails on deck, where it had been hosed down by the spray coming aft at 30 knots. The wind shifted again almost as soon as that sail was up and pulling, the angle tightening a few more degrees. With Fernando de Noronha just ahead, they couldn't afford to be forced off their course. The boat speed started to dip, and the R1 was pulled up, another slightly smaller sail.

Barely was the R1 hoisted and set when the news arrived on deck that there was an inbound squall on the radar. Before another hour had passed it was blowing 30 knots, and Poortman was back on the bow struggling to get the sodden R1 into its bag with the smaller-still J4 now flying. There was no time to draw breath as they heaved the sail aft and back into the stack. This blast of breeze was just on the front edge of the squall, and it was already starting to ease. They were going to need a bigger sail.

The demands were constant on the whole crew, the watch system having effectively been suspended by force of circumstances. There was no rhythm or pattern to the workload. The J4 came down and up went the R2,

but not for long. Soon the sun was poking through the cloud at the back of the squall, sending dazzling rainbows into the spray kicked up by the bow. It was time to haul the code zero back out from under the hundreds of kilograms of wet sailcloth that had been dumped on top of it. They had come full circle, and then the whole sequence, or some variation of it, began again. In all, Poortman reckoned that Delta Lloyd changed sails close to 30 times in the 12 hours before the scoring gate.

If that wasn't tough enough, on the final approach in the darkness their boat speed suddenly plunged; there was a big, unseen hole in the breeze by the island of Fernando de Noronha. They changed gear and sailed on, almost there and still in third. Then they realised that a red light coming towards them was PUMA. And she was very, very close. Ken Read and his team had sailed around the light spot and made huge gains. The crew of Delta Lloyd watched anxiously as the two boats closed on an apparent collision course. Finally, Poortman scrambled up to the bow to make the call on whether they were far enough ahead to cross in front. They were, and just over 400 metres short of the scoring gate, Delta Lloyd got their boat between PUMA and the line, holding third place by just over 100 metres.

At the scoring gate, Telefónica Blue and Ericsson 4 had taken first and second, while PUMA was chased across the line by Telefónica Black, Ericsson 3 and finally Green Dragon. Just over two and a half hours separated second from sixth. Initially, conditions improved as they escaped north from Fernando de Noronha and turned northwest towards Boston, but they still had to transit the Doldrums one final time for this race. It had been a graveyard of ambition before – in the 1993–94 race, Lawrie Smith's dreams of an overall win with the Whitbread 60 Intrum Justitia had disappeared in the Doldrums en route to Fort Lauderdale. And just hours after the scoring gate, Ericsson 4's second-place advantage dissolved in warm Atlantic rainwater as she got badly caught in a cloud. By midday on 17 April, there were only four miles between second and sixth, and battle commenced to clear the Doldrums first.

Bouwe Bekking, Jordi Calafat, Jonathan Swain and the rest aboard Telefónica Blue escaped unscathed, quickly breaking through into the northeast trade winds. Their lead rocketed to over 100 miles in the 24 hours after the scoring gate. Behind them, it was a very different matter, and at the end of the same period there were still only 10 miles separating second to sixth. But the others were finally moving, and beginning to make up ground on the leader. Once again, it was steady trade-wind boat-speed sailing, but the northeast trade winds were strong. And in those conditions, Green Dragon and Delta Lloyd were slowly left behind by the two Ericsson boats, Telefónica Black and PUMA.

One by one, the yachts all crossed their outbound track from Alicante as they raced north from Fernando de Noronha. There was some discussion over whether this constituted a complete circumnavigation. The general view was no, but one man who had unequivocally completed his trip around the world was PUMA's Australian shore manager, Neil Cox. The team had prepared and trained in the Boston area. The boat had departed for Alicante and the start of the Volvo Ocean

left PUMA's shore manager, Neil Cox (bottom: left of picture, guiding the crane driver in Qingdao), was responsible for 16 people on the shore team. Their tasks ranged from giving the boat its final wash before it went back in the water (top: ahead of the leg start from Rio), to cooking 100 meals a day for the shore team, crew and families. The team completed its own circumnavigation at the end of leg six, having started from Boston to sail to Alicante.

Race from just down the coast at Newport, Rhode Island. Cox had followed them round the world on aeroplanes, and now, landing at Boston's Logan International Airport, he had returned to his starting point.

Their sponsors, PUMA, had offices and personnel in Boston, and many came down to say hello both before, and after, the boat's arrival. The team had a container out at the airport on Aquidneck Island, where the boat's spare daggerboards, rudders and other gear was stored. And Cox, along with many of the team's itinerant workforce, had stored personal belongings with Sean Healy, the team's electrical and electronics engineer. Healy was the owner of a large family home that currently had a basement full of other people's belongings. Everything else had gone on the journey with them, along with two full sets of equipment, which had leapfrogged each other around the world. One set, landed in North America by the race's official logistics partner, Wallenius Wilhelmsen, had come from Qingdao and would go no further. The second set was on its way from Rio to Galway, and would be used for all three of the final stopovers.

Each set included all the spares and equipment that they needed to run the team, and service and maintain the yacht. Like rope: 1.5 kilometres of it were used to sail the boat, and all of it might be replaced three or four times during the race. So it had to be on hand in places like China and India where there were no local suppliers. Then there were the big-ticket items, like cradles for the yacht when it was out of the water; spare and used sails; a generator; two workshop containers with tools; one storage container; two office containers and equipment; along with everything that was needed

to construct the tented boatbuilding, kitchen and dining areas, and the sail loft, with its two industrial sewing machines. There was even an eight-metre electric scissor lift that could shift 800-kilogram loads around the shore base. All of this equipment had to be turned into a functioning shore base at the Race Village in Fan Pier, Boston; and then the 1,600 hours or more of labour for the 11 people that would prepare PUMA for leg seven had to be planned. Despite the satisfaction of arriving back at what currently passed for home, Cox had no time to dwell on it.

There was little time for introspection for Cox's team-mates aboard PUMA either, still neck and neck with Telefónica Black and the two Ericsson boats, chasing Telefónica Blue northwards in the trade winds. Then disaster struck for Roger Nilson and the team on Telefónica Black. Early in the morning of 19 April, Nilson was in his bunk when the boat hit something, slowing from 21 knots to eight knots in less than a second. On deck, Spanish sail trimmer David Vera and skipper Fernando Echávarri were both knocked off their feet. The boat spun into the wind and slowed to a stop. And a whale surfaced on the starboard side. It was an awful moment, as Echávarri wrote afterwards: *"Everyone onboard loves the sea and its animals, and it has been a real shock to hit one of them."* Telefónica Black was lucky; although there was some play in the keel bearings, and cracks in the fairing of the bulb and fin, no one was hurt. Then, a few hours after the incident, a fitting started to break repeatedly on the headsail, almost certainly overstressed by the collision. It took a couple of hours to fix and the whole episode dropped Telefónica Black

above Ericsson 4's media crew, Guy Salter, wrote about the frustrations of photographing wildlife from a racing yacht: *"We have seen eight turtles in the last two hours and I have been trying to get pictures of them, but as soon as you press the record button and wait for the red light to say everything is go, you've passed them by. Then I was told I had missed the* whale ... *I asked if anyone had picked up the camera and filmed it — but no one had, even though I had left everything ready ... Just heard we have had some dolphins visit while I've been writing this — so much for my lookouts!"* This one, at least, didn't get away — but the picture was taken by Green Dragon's media crew, Guo Chuan.

down from third place to join Delta Lloyd and Green Dragon at the back of the fleet.

Aboard Ericsson 4, English navigator Jules Salter had settled into his own trade-wind routine. Independent of the watch system that dominated the lives of eight of his crewmates, his own existence was driven by the weather forecasts arriving on their six-hourly cycle at midnight, 06.00, 12.00 and 18.00 GMT. He would be wide awake and awaiting the arrival of each new set of forecast files, checking the forecast charts as soon as they started to download on to his computer. After that, the computer simulations would start, using the programmed mathematical algorithms to race a virtual Volvo Open 70 through the computerised files.

Salter automatically graphed the actual weather conditions too, and he compared this record with the forecast, looking for variations that might give further clues to how things would develop. This took at least an hour, by which time the position report would be landing in his inbox. Sent out by the duty officer at Race HQ every three hours on the schedule 01.00, 04.00, 07.00, 10.00, 13.00, 16.00, 19.00 and 22.00 GMT, this contained information on the position of each yacht in the fleet, along with her wind speed and direction. It was effectively a real-time weather report for the area of ocean that the fleet covered. It provided further valuable corroboration, or otherwise, of the conditions in the forecast received an hour earlier.

All this new data had to be processed and analysed, distributed to the skipper, watch captains and crew, and the tactical implications assessed. Those discussions might take minutes or hours, depending on the complexity of the situation. Only when they were done would Salter try and get his head down for some sleep, usually leaving skipper Torben Grael to review the next position report, while he snatched a couple of hours before the whole process started again. In the northeast trade winds it was a steady routine. Interruptions like sail changes, manoeuvres or approaching squalls sighted on the radar were relatively few and far between. And Salter started to focus on the major strategic play of the leg.

The fleet was sailing northwest and slowly coming under the influence of the Azores High, a semi-permanent area of high pressure that drifted around the North Atlantic. Telefónica Blue was leading the fleet out of the trade winds and into the lighter wind in the high, and, as a consequence, her advantage was slowly disappearing. By the morning of 21 April, it was down to 30 miles and dropping. Skipper Bouwe Bekking wrote from the boat:
"We have been on the receiving end now for roughly 36 hours, losing mile after mile, which is part of the game. I don't think it will stop for at least another 20 hours, as then finally the others will hit the wall as well ... we are fully preparing ourselves for a re-start."

The gap closed to 20 miles before everyone was north of the trade winds, and a new weather system began to dominate the strategy. A cold front was approaching from the west, and the accompanying wind shift meant that they would have to gybe to transit the front and stay on course for Boston. The timing would be crucial, and it was this move that Salter and all the other navigators were focused on. The pace

above Everyone uses some sort of eye protection when it's wet and windy. Ski goggles are popular, but the disadvantage is that the foam protection round the edges can freeze, making the skin swell. Windsurfing helmets with visors were also popular, and some sailors experimented with triathlon swim goggles.

picked up as the wind increased and shifted, and the spinnakers were hoisted. These were Ericsson 4's favourite conditions; although not quite the record-breaking breeze of leg one, it still provided the kind of sailing in which she had always dominated. In the 24 hours between the mornings of 22 and 23 April, the crew jumped their boat across that final 20-mile gap, leaving Ericsson 3 and PUMA behind, and closing to within a handful of miles of Telefónica Blue.

At 07.00 GMT on the morning of 23 April, Bouwe Bekking called in a StealthPlay to the Race Office and gybed his boat. The StealthPlay rules meant that Telefónica Blue was removed from the next 12 hours of position reports issued by the Race Office.

It broke the pattern of steady information and left Salter and Grael to guess at their opponent's strategy. Now they couldn't stay close to Telefónica Blue and rely on their speed to get past. Salter returned to his calculations. They waited until just after the 10.00 GMT position report, then gybed in a position 80 miles north of Telefónica Blue. Torben Grael called in Ericsson 4's StealthPlay at the same time, and everyone watching around the world held their breath to see who had got it right, and who had got it wrong.

Aboard Telefónica Blue they already knew the answer. The lead they had won in the land breeze off Brazil evaporated completely as they ran out of wind just hours after the gybe. Ericsson 4 went past them at the 10.00 GMT position report, before Grael's boat even disappeared into Stealth. From there it just got worse. When the cloaks were all lifted, it emerged that Telefónica Blue had been 20 miles behind Ericsson 4 at 13.00 GMT, by 16.00 GMT they were 30 miles back and

into third behind Ericsson 3, and by 19.00 GMT the deficit to the leader was 50 miles and they were fourth behind PUMA. But Bouwe Bekking wasn't hiding from their error. Reflecting on an earlier email, he wrote from the boat:

"I said it a couple of days ago: 'You gybe too early and you run out of pressure ... That will be the race call.' Well, we gybed too early, no excuse, it is a huge f***-up. The reality was that we couldn't hold off Ericsson 4, they were sailing much faster than us last night, but by gybing too early we lost against the rest of the fleet."

And with that, the crew of Telefónica Blue settled down to fight back from another steep drop on their roller-coaster ride.

There was still plenty of opportunity. Sailing northwest, the fleet was moving against the flow of weather systems coming off the North American continent. The changes were coming ever faster, combined with the complexity of crossing the swirling Gulf Stream current, which rushes northeast up the Atlantic seaboard of the US. But even apart from all this, there was something that could give Telefónica Blue and the others hope. Ericsson 4 had a serious problem; media crew Guy Salter reported it on the evening of 23 April: *"In the middle of all our cloak and dagger tactics of the StealthPlay we had a disaster on board Ericsson 4. We discovered – or I should say Phil [Jameson] discovered – that we had an issue with our watermaker."*

Boat captain David Endean knew the problem was bad as soon as he saw it. The water rapidly gathering in the bilge of the engine box didn't have the smell of engine coolant, nor was the engine overheating. There was only one other place it could be coming from, and that was the watermaker. The unit worked by forcing sea water at high pressure (5.5 bar), through a 1.5-metre tube filled with a membrane that filtered out the salt and other impurities. Drinking water emerged from the other end: but not any more. The pressure had found some kind of flaw in the plastic cap and blown a hole in the side of it big enough to push your thumb into. It was clearly impossible to seal the hole. Nothing they had on board would stay in place against a pressure more than five times the atmosphere's. And they had no spare.

Afterwards, Endean reflected that it was impossible to carry a spare for everything on board, and as he had used the unit on two previous races without a single problem, this was the last thing he had expected to fail. But it had. And it left them three days out from the finish with just 30 litres of water in the tank. Guy Salter wrote, *"We have immediately banned coffee and tea and our meals will be significantly reduced. We have decided on a dangerously low 1.5 litres per person to drink and have separated up each quota into a bottle which the individual will be responsible for."* It wasn't going to be fun, but they could get to the finish. If it had happened a week earlier they would have been done for, forced to pull in and pick up a spare, losing at least 12 hours and almost certainly finishing in last place. It was a short sharp reminder that despite their big lead, the race was a long way from over.

The conditions crossing the Gulf Stream were reminiscent of leg four's encounter with the Kuroshio. The northwesterly wind was blowing against the current at 20 to 30 knots with gusts up to 40 knots, producing some boat-breaking waves 10 metres high.

But it was a shorter and milder hammering, and this time the whole fleet emerged intact into a dramatically different world: grey, cold water, cool air and fast-dropping wind speed. The fleet made a sudden lurch to the west, as everyone realised it was the best way around a barrier of high pressure and light wind growing like Jack's beanstalk between them and Boston.

The leaders hit it first and slowed almost to a halt. Telefónica Blue passed PUMA and caught Ericsson 3. Then they separated again to look for a final push from the last of the Gulf Stream current, only to see the Nordic crew sail away from them. Worse, the Ericsson 3 crew played their Stealth card and reappeared on the morning of 25 April just two miles behind Ericsson 4. Jordi Calafat commented ruefully afterwards, "In the whole Volvo we sailed a little bit too loose, leaving the fleet and getting to the corners ... and we paid the price, especially on this leg."

Aboard Ericsson 4, the appearance of Ericsson 3 right on their transom meant that they had no trouble focusing, even if making a cup of coffee had become something of an ordeal. Horacio Carabelli, Brazilian sail trimmer, reported from the boat:

"My right arm is getting bigger and bigger! We started using the hand watermaker and the only way Nipper [Guy Salter] *will allow you to have a coffee is if you pump your own water into the kettle ... You need to pump 180 times to get one cup of coffee, and if you offer to make coffee for your watch mates, it will take you 25 minutes."*

If the "sail changing world championships" had broken the watch systems as the fleet approached the scoring gate, this time it was the rapid passage of

weather fronts that trashed the routine for the skippers and navigators. The constant demands from the changing conditions meant that Jules Salter slept for a single hour in the final two days – and this on the meagre fuel provided by just one meal and a litre and a half of water a day. Nonetheless, the Ericsson 4 team still had the answers when the game was tight, leading out of the ridge of high pressure and into a freshening southwesterly wind – although they were chased hard by their sister ship.

The fleet closed on an exclusion zone that had been set up by Race management to keep them away from the whales of the Stellwagen Bank National Marine Sanctuary. PUMA emerged from her own StealthPlay metres in front of Telefónica Blue, just as they reached the whale exclusion-zone. Behind them, Delta Lloyd had taken a chance on a more easterly route, but was holding off Telefónica Black, while Green Dragon was still struggling for speed at the back. And that might have been how it ended. The whale exclusion-zone meant the final miles were sailed down a narrow southwesterly corridor between the zone and the New England coastline. It could have been a straightforward procession, but as Ericsson 4 turned the northern corner of the exclusion zone into the home straight, she hit yet another weather system. It was a weak cold front. The wind shifted to the northwest and became very light. Ericsson 4 just held off Ericsson 3, finishing only 12 minutes ahead. But Telefónica Blue got the better of PUMA in the transition to earn a crucial extra point (enough to put them into second place overall) and almost caught the Nordics, only five minutes adrift on the line.

Behind them, Telefónica Black's return to the race had been derailed by the collision. There was scant consolation in catching Delta Lloyd in the light winds as they sailed around the extra miles of the whale exclusion-zone. Both boats had surged back into the race on a wave of energy and enthusiasm, but circumstance (the collision) and fundamental issues (an old boat, a lack of training time) had limited the impact that they had been able to make. In the end, the status quo had remained intact, but a question had been asked of the future.

In Rio, Ken Read had commented, "This race is brutal to human beings. There is no doubt in my mind that next time everybody will be rotating way more just because of the nature of the game. If it was for the good of the team, I'd rotate myself." And Bouwe Bekking had written from the boat during leg six:
"It also shows that having three fresh guys on board has lifted our strength and spirits and in that sense it is good to know that we have a recovered 'Iker' [co-skipper Iker Martínez had decided to rest for leg six] *back in Boston. It will mean somebody has to step off, not always a nice thing, as everybody likes to sail every leg. But I can clearly see what advantages it has and only the team result will count and nobody should feel bad if the choice falls on him."*

Nevertheless, despite Bannatyne's earlier concerns about tiredness, the crew of Ericsson 4 had not been found wanting, even with the added disadvantage of the broken watermaker. Whatever the race had thrown at them – re-energised competitors, StealthPlays, frenetic sail changes or fast-moving weather systems – they hadn't missed a stride. The debate would rage on, but no one could deny that the unchanged crew of

Ericsson 4, with their long months of training, seemed better able to cope with the surprises and the broken rhythms of the race's myriad demands than those teams that had tried to match that fast pace of change with change of their own. As Torben Grael explained, "This time we have had the luxury of practising for almost a year. Your problems should come in that period and not the race. The advantage is we don't want surprises in how people behave and sail. And no one is afraid of being dropped. There are many advantages."

Once again the day of the in-port race dawned grey, with the wind speed struggling to get into double figures. It should have been Ken Read's turn to dazzle the home-town crowd, but the Boston University alumnus had a day more reminiscent of Torben Grael's grim experience in Rio than Telefónica Blue's golden performance in Alicante. PUMA finished sixth after a three-way tie-break. It was a result that was compounded by Bouwe Bekking and his team continuing their run of in-port-race success. Telefónica Blue added another win to move three points clear of PUMA overall. Ericsson 4 recovered brilliantly after crossing the start line prematurely to take second for the day, maintaining a 12.5-point overall lead. It ought to be enough, just so long as there were no more ticking time bombs, like the watermaker, hiding away in the complex systems that the crew of Ericsson 4 depended on in so many different ways.

left Delta Lloyd approaches the finish of leg six, right in front of the city of Boston, on a beautiful summer afternoon. But it was a moment of disappointment for the crew; they were passed by Telefónica Black in the final miles.

Collision Crossing

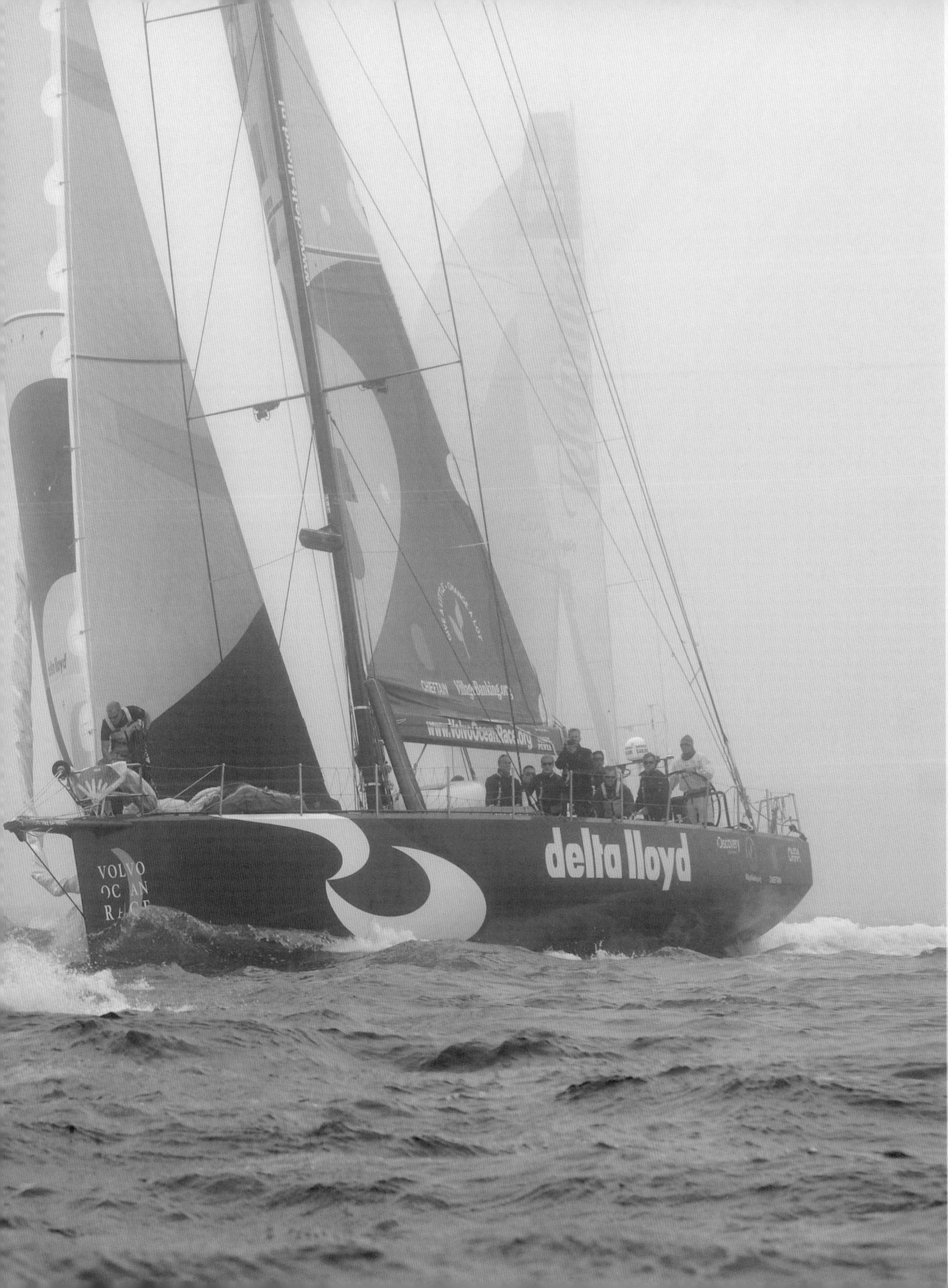

chapter opener Ericsson 4 and Delta Lloyd duel in the Boston Harbor fog at the start of leg seven. Delta Lloyd later had to take evasive action when a merchant ship suddenly emerged from the fog.

The cold, grim conditions were made even grimmer by the third anniversary of the loss of Hans Horrevoets, which occurred during the leg. Delta Lloyd's bowman, Gerd-Jan Poortman, marked the day by writing to Hans's parents and his wife, Petra. He was far from alone in thinking of Hans that day.

The Race management announced a new trophy: the Hans Horrevoets Rookie Award, to be awarded to the race's top rookie sailor (defined as under 30 when the race commenced) by race officials, selecting from the skippers' nominations. It was the under-30 crew of ABN AMRO TWO that Horrevoets had helped to select, then coached and eventually sailed with, until the tragic events of 18 May 2006.

left Ken Read steers PUMA away from the start of leg seven.

Time was running out for the crews of Telefónica Blue and PUMA – time and available points. If they were to challenge Ericsson 4 all the way to the finish, they needed a result on leg seven. It was the classic transatlantic crossing: 2,550 miles from Boston to Galway on the west coast of Ireland. There were reasons for the pursuing teams to be hopeful: risk of strategic error or gear failure was omnipresent, as leg six had demonstrated. And previous Atlantic legs had always seen more than their fair share of close calls and broken dreams, perhaps because it was close to the end, and the boats and their crews were tired.

The most famous close call was aboard Steinlager2 in 1989–90. The big red ketch of legendary skipper Peter Blake had dominated the event, winning all of the first five legs. Then, four days out from Fort Lauderdale and bound for the race finish in Southampton, rigging that held both masts aloft had given way. Only an instant reaction on the wheel had saved them, gybing the boat to transfer the rig loads to the other side; that, and a full night of repair work, got them home in one piece and first place, to complete an epic six-leg sweep.

The conditions at the start in Boston couldn't have been more ominous either, as fog rolled in across the harbour. But despite a ship looming out of the murk just metres in front of Delta Lloyd, and a close call with a powerboat for Telefónica Blue, the tightly grouped boats all escaped into open water intact. The course was eastwards, past Nova Scotia and around the tip of the Grand Banks of Newfoundland. It is here that the icy waters of the Labrador Current flow south from the Arctic and meet the warm water carried north from the tropics by the Gulf Stream. A high-pressure system was guiding warm air from the south over the cold water to create the fog.

The southerly wind made for fast sailing, but with a high risk of collision as they crossed busy shipping lanes and the fertile feeding grounds of the Grand Banks. Green Dragon's skipper, Ian Walker, wrote prophetically about the hazard as they left Boston: *"I think fog is one of the worst hazards at sea, and for Ian [Moore, navigator] and I, it will mean a 24-hour radar watch. Radar doesn't help much with lobster pots though, so we will need a bit of Irish luck to help out there."*

But luck was absent for the Dragon's English watch captain Neal McDonald, at the wheel on the morning of 17 May, as the fleet approached Cape Sable at the southern tip of Nova Scotia. The fact that Lobster Bay lay to the north of them was a warning – using a lookout on the bow, McDonald reckoned that they dodged 50 to 60 lobster pots within three hours. Then, just a quarter-mile short of the end of the lobster field, Green Dragon picked up three, one of which cut its way 300 millimetres into the front edge of the daggerboard.

Neal McDonald didn't have a good record on the Atlantic. His three attempts at record runs had ended in failure, due to a broken daggerboard, a hull problem and a damaged rudder. He knew that water pressure over Green Dragon's daggerboard would now force apart the components of the structure until they failed. They set about fixing it, while others swapped the second, still functional daggerboard into its place. It took a couple of hours, and by the time the boat was back to performing at 100 per cent they were 20 miles off the lead. The repair took longer; they had to clean the wound, fill it with space-age gloop and then lay carbon-fibre patches

Jens Dolmer puts on his safety harness. There is a strobe light attached to his right shoulder for visibility at night should he go overboard. Dolmer is wearing a thin fleece balaclava; the final touches to clothing are important, and quite personal. Some sailors wear a neck scarf, a fleece tube that goes over the top of the neck seal on the survival suit or smock and covers the gap to the beanie. Neoprene gloves aren't good against wind chill, but still allow for some feel in the fingers to work with ropes or fiddly hardware. The cuffs on the smock or survival suit fold down over the end of the gloves so water doesn't run down your arms.

right Eduard van Lierde starts to get suited up for a stint on deck. He's wearing at least one thermal layer next to the skin, with boots and foul-weather trousers the next to go on; a jacket will follow. On the wall behind him are safety instructions for abandoning ship. It was on the transatlantic leg in the previous race in 2005–06 that the yacht movistar had to be abandoned.

over the top for strength. The board was back in place at first light the following morning.

The fleet had reached Cape Sable within half a mile of each other, but Delta Lloyd had also struggled with the pace as the race eastwards heated up for the points at the scoring gate. The gate ran south from St John's, Newfoundland, down the line of longitude 52 deg 38 min W. Ericsson 3 slowly eased out in front, taking a narrow lead from PUMA and Telefónica Blue on the afternoon of 17 May. They maintained it overnight, the wind getting lighter and shifting to the southeast, slowing everyone down – something for which the crew of Ericsson 3 was about to be grateful.

It was not long after sunrise and media crew Gustav Morin was writing his daily blog:
"At the moment we are going slowly. We have 12 knots of wind ... making 10 knots of boat speed through a thick never-seem-to-be-ending fog ... S***!! Just when I was writing this we hit a whale. I just heard bowman Anders Dahlsjö shouting from deck, 'I think we are sailing over a whale just now!' And seconds later, bambambam! It felt just like we went aground."

Martin Krite was off-watch, trying to sleep, and was hurled forwards into the next bunk. His initial reaction was to conclude that they had hit some of the ice flowing south in the Labrador Current, but the shouts from on deck made clear what had actually happened: they had collided with a whale estimated to be as big as Ericsson 3 by those who got the best view of it. The animal dived; boat captain Jens Dolmer checked the structure and concluded that the damage wasn't serious. Krite and the off-watch were returning to their

bunks before they had even got up on deck. The race for the scoring-gate points went on.

They may have sustained no structural damage, but Ericsson 3 soon began a steady slide down the rankings. And once darkness crept around them on the evening of 18 May, Krite and the others noticed a marked increase in the phosphorescence in the wake of the boat. It was created by damage suffered by the foils in the collision, and it was also slowing them down. Initially, PUMA took over the lead, but Telefónica Blue was on a charge. The wind had increased a little, and Ken Read and his team changed to a smaller sail. By the time they were done, the boats were side by side. The wind was blowing from the beam at such a speed and angle that both boats were close to delivering a knockout punch. The turbulent air thrown off the sails at this angle to the wind extended out from both sides of the boat. If either skipper could get far enough forward, they could starve the other of clean breeze, cutting off their opponent's power supply and jumping to an uncontested lead.

For the last three hours the two crews, separated by just three points in the overall standings, sailed as though it were an inshore race. Each time the killer blow was launched, the other wriggled clear to fight on. But someone had to be in front when the bell rang and they hit the line of the scoring gate. It was so close that the Race Office asked the media crews to film the onboard GPS receivers showing position and time as they crossed. Just 40 seconds separated the two boats, and it was Telefónica Blue that once again got the win. Ever the bridesmaid, it seemed that Ken Read's PUMA couldn't quite produce the final 0.5 per cent to get to the top step of the podium.

Behind them, Ericsson 4 took third, Ericsson 3 fourth, then Telefónica Black, Delta Lloyd and Green Dragon.

Along with the last three boats through the scoring gate, Ericsson 4 had realised early that they couldn't better their position at the scoring gate. They had added a southerly component into their course to clear an ice exclusion zone (IEZ), which had been created to keep the fleet clear of the ice flowing south in the Labrador Current. And now, as Telefónica Blue, PUMA and Ericsson 3 finally diverted to the south as well, it turned the leader board on its head. Telefónica Black moved to the front, with Green Dragon reducing a 40-mile deficit to pass Ericsson 3. But when the sun rose on 19 May, and Martin Krite and the crew finally got a proper look at the damage to their daggerboard, it confirmed the other reason for their fall from first to last. They were able to change it for the spare – which every crew (except Green Dragon) had carried since both Telefónica boats had broken them in leg two. There was nothing they could do about the keel fin. It would slow them all the way to the finish (just as it had for Telefónica Black on the previous leg), and thanks to the whale a run of fine results would come to an end with a last place.

Telefónica Black held her advantage to the southwestern corner of the IEZ, where the fleet was able to head east again, along the southern limit. There were signs of the Gulf Stream, and as they hit the swirls of warmer water, the conditions miraculously changed. Black maintained her moment of glory until the southeastern corner, but by then she had the three top boats right on her tail. And the game, like the weather as they hit the Gulf Stream, was about to change.

The classic transatlantic crossing would normally see the fleet swept from west to east with a low-pressure system. But so far the leg had been dominated by southerly winds, straight-line sailing and cloying fog. Now, a big Atlantic low-pressure system was inbound from the northwest, dragging a cold front with it. Ericsson 4 was soon revelling in her favourite conditions as the fleet set spinnakers away from the IEZ. It didn't take her long to blow past Telefónica Black, who was hampered by an unfortunate turtle that had got itself lodged on the keel, forcing the crew to stop so the turtle could swim free. If it was out there, the Volvo Open 70s could hit it! But worse was to come, as Telefónica Black's navigator, Roger Nilson, wrote from the boat: *"Soon we realised that both Telefónica Blue and PUMA were considerably faster than us. We had to watch PUMA passing us effortlessly, going more than a knot faster and a few degrees lower under her biggest masthead gennaker in 27 knots of cold air."*

They may have been quicker, but aboard Telefónica Blue it was anything but effortless. Watch captain Jonathan Swain later reported that they were double-teaming in an effort to finally tame the beast downwind. They had six men on deck instead of four, with an extra man helping on the winch for both the mainsail and spinnaker. It meant a watch system of six hours on and two off, but they were finally competitive in the conditions that had been their weakness since the first transit of the Atlantic, seven months earlier.

The morning of 21 May dawned with an ominous red sky and a line of cloud building from the west: 'Red sky in morning, sailor's warning'. Aboard Green Dragon, Neal McDonald had a bad feeling; the weather had the same ugly look as it had on the transatlantic leg of the

left Green Dragon's skipper, Ian Walker, peers out of the hatch to check conditions on deck ... and it's still cold, wet and grey. The sailors endured freezing conditions on this leg as they sailed across the Labrador Current, which flows south from the Arctic. Cold water and southerly winds meant freezing fog, poor visibility and the constant risk of collision. It combined with the intense competition to ensure that this was a very stressful period. The demands of a seven-day leg, or even a two-day leg, could be just as great as for the six-week epic of leg five.

above **Most boats during the 2008–09 race left the boat's time set to GMT, so that it matched the time at the Race Office. Then, as they sailed eastwards, the time on board would gradually move out of sync with the actual sunrise and sunset. Graveyard shifts eventually became dawn patrols, and breakfast was eaten at lunchtime, so meals had to be swapped every few days.**

previous race. Of more immediate concern to Ericsson 4's navigator, Jules Salter, was how to balance the preferred weather strategy with the desire to play the fleet. Behind them, the chasing pack reshuffled itself several times as they sailed away from the IEZ, the position reports painting a confusing picture.

The other skippers knew what they were doing, timing their gybes to make it hard to judge how they planned to tackle the low. But Ericsson 4 was fast approaching the cold front and Salter had to make a decision. In the early afternoon, the Race Office received an email from Guy Salter, Ericsson 4's media crew: *"The fleet looks to have split, so Jules is running and rerunning routes to check we are happy heading north before it's too late to consolidate some of our position."* By the time it was received, Ericsson 4 had broken through the front and was pointing at Galway in a gale of breeze and a vicious seaway. There was no going back. Ericsson 3 and Green Dragon followed Ericsson 4 northwards, and also crossed the front at the first opportunity. But the real opposition, Telefónica Blue and PUMA, stayed south, the other side of the cold front, racing in a pack with Telefónica Black and Delta Lloyd. Sailing in different winds, the fleet rapidly diverged.

By the early evening the two groups were 100 miles apart, and conditions had markedly deteriorated for the crew on Ericsson 4. Guy Salter explained how they tried to deal with it:
"Most of the boys out here, and definitely all onboard Ericsson 4, are very much in control of their emotions – you don't want to get too excited by the highs and you don't want to open yourself up to the lows. This emotional guarding is often seen as arrogance, or the boys are judged as boring, when in reality it's just an adaptation for us to be able to push hard and be competitive in extreme conditions that would otherwise see people fold. The alarms ringing out in the brain are carefully analysed and ignored in pursuit of performance."

The 11 men aboard PUMA were about to have their emotions severely tested. Rick Deppe was in his bunk, thinking that it was about time he got up and put the evening meal on, when he heard a huge bang and the boat immediately lurched out of control. Deppe dived for the "crash button", which automatically saves the last two minutes of images from the on-deck cameras. Then he grabbed the hand-held video camera and powered it up, just in time to catch English watch captain Rob Greenhalgh as he clambered out of the stern. He confirmed for Deppe that they had snapped a rudder off just six inches below the hull.

The navigator, Andrew Cape, now appeared on deck clutching his gear bag, saying that the last time he'd heard a bang that loud in this part of the world, it had been time to get off. Cape had been aboard movistar, abandoned not far from this same spot in the previous race; some thought the joke funnier than others did. But almost immediately PUMA got some help from the weather. They had gybed to bring the undamaged starboard rudder into use, and not long after that the cold front caught up with them. It poured with rain, the wind shifted to the west and now they were going the right way while they worked on the repair.

Telefónica Black had snapped a rudder in leg one, and they had limped to Cape Town with the emergency spare hung off the back of the boat. But PUMA had a different plan; it was an idea of their former watch *right* The PUMA crew replaces their broken rudder during leg seven. The images were taken from Rick Deppe's Inmarsat Media Prize–winning video footage, and run from top left to bottom right. First, the old rudder is knocked out of its shaft running through the hull, with a rope attached to the top of the rudder stock, so the rope ends up trailing out of the bottom of the rudder shaft. The old rudder is retrieved and the rope transferred to the top of the stock of the replacement rudder. Casey Smith is then dangled over the side of the boat and the new rudder passed down to him. From the deck, the rest of the crew pull on the rope running through the rudder shaft and, with Smith guiding it, the new rudder slots neatly into place. The repair won Smith the Wallenius Wilhelmsen Logistics Seamanship Award.

captain, Chris Nicholson, who had been unable to continue racing after he snapped an anterior cruciate ligament in leg two. PUMA's emergency rudder had been specially modified to allow it to replace the broken one, rather than be deployed on the transom like Telefónica Black's. It was a secret weapon, but they still had to make it work. Rick Deppe filmed bowman and boat captain Casey Smith as he was dangled over and into the freezing North Atlantic, helping to guide the new rudder into place. The execution of the repair won Smith the Wallenius Wilhelmsen Logistics Seamanship Award, and the film helped Deppe win his third Inmarsat Media Prize. More importantly, a little over two hours after the damage they were back up and running as though nothing had happened – although Neil Cox was going to have to fetch one of those spare rudders he had stored back in New England.

The cold front had caught and swept over the other three southern boats while PUMA's crew were wrestling to fix their rudder, and they had all gybed with her. The whole fleet was now headed northeast, with over 100 miles of north-to-south separation, or leverage, between the two groups. Conditions remained fierce. Gerd-Jan Poortman later described an oh-God-hold-on moment aboard Delta Lloyd. They came down the face of one wave so fast there was nothing the helmsman could do; they just speared straight into the back of the one in front. Poortman was working the big winch pedestal at the time. He heard the shouted warning from the helmsman and dropped to the deck and gripped the pedestal in a bear hug. The bow went in and the water poured back in a foaming wave.

Poortman held his breath and hung on, the water over his head and the world green and white. To keep the weight as far back as possible the two other crew on deck were sitting in the stern, and as soon as he surfaced, Poortman glanced back and then gave the helmsman a thumbs up to tell him that everyone was still on the boat. The next thing Poortman was aware of was the spinnaker flogging – the force of the impact into the wave had blown the front of the sail apart. Down below, the off-watch was already tumbling out of the bunks to help get the sail down.

All through the evening of 21 May and into the 22nd, the navigators braced themselves into position at their posts, trying to focus tired eyes on bouncing computer screens as the boats in which they sat were hurled from one wave to another by the crew on deck. The fleet's separation would play out in one final strategic move before Galway. As the low-pressure system moved away from the fleet to the northeast, another was approaching from the southwest. The combination shifted the wind back towards the south, forcing the fleet to gybe to reach the finish.

Green Dragon was pushing up to and sometimes beyond the limit, desperate for a good result into her home port. The line that held the big fractional zero sail to the bowsprit snapped, and the metal furler scythed around on the end of a 29-metre-long wire. Before the crew could get it under control, the lower part of the sail was trashed so badly it was impossible to repair it on board. Fortunately, that was the only damage, and afterwards Neal McDonald reckoned that the small spinnaker they put up instead encouraged them to gybe a little earlier than they might have otherwise – and that turned out to be no bad thing.

One by one, as the evening turned to night, the skippers called in their StealthPlays, the boats disappeared from the position reports and the gybes followed. When the sun came up on the morning of 23 May, the fleet reappeared and the situation was fully revealed: with 500 miles to sail almost due east to Galway, the boats were spread out north-to-south over 125 miles of the North Atlantic. They had to converge – but who would come out in front? The northern route paid. By the middle of the afternoon Ericsson 4 had moved across in front of everyone and grabbed a 40-mile lead. It was another dominant performance; playing the fleet or working the weather, there was no doubt who was top dog.

Green Dragon had also passed the entire southern group, with PUMA recovering from the broken rudder to get back up into third after Telefónica Blue left her gybe a little too late. It was a potentially costly error: in the battle for second overall every point counted. The wind now continued its shift towards the south and stayed strong, and Green Dragon started to suffer for want of the sail they had broken. Ian Walker reported:
"We have clung on to our bigger spinnaker right on the edge of control ... It has taken two extra guys on deck to keep up with the constant trimming. Now the wind has shifted and we can use a reaching headsail so we are less on a knife edge. One would expect the faster reaching boats to pull us in, but maybe they have difficulties too? Can they catch us quickly enough?"

When everyone finally fell into line astern and closed out the leverage, Ericsson 4 was almost across the finish line. The leg win was secured soon afterwards, and with it, in all but the maths, the race. Behind them,

PUMA had a second-place lead of a couple of miles, and the focus of the big crowds gathering dockside in Galway now shifted on to whether the Dragon could hold off the renewed charge of Telefónica Blue. The reaching conditions favoured the Spanish boat, and Bouwe Bekking and his team needed to avoid losing the extra point. They cut the lead at a rate of one mile per hour, but they ran out of racetrack. PUMA finished second, with Green Dragon third and on the podium into their home port. Telefónica Blue was fourth, with a gap of just over 11 minutes between the two pairs of boats; while behind them, Delta Lloyd, Telefónica Black and Ericsson 3 filed home over the next three hours.

The reception for the fleet was extraordinary but the best was saved for Ian Walker, Neal McDonald and the rest of the Green Dragon crew, matching anything McDonald had seen in his professional career. And by hanging on to third, Green Dragon more than delighted the boisterous Saturday-night crowd.

Ericsson 4's win had given them a 14.5-point lead, and even though it was cut to 13 after an average performance in the subsequent in-port racing, everyone recognised that Torben Grael, Jules Salter, Stu Bannatyne, David Endean and the rest of the team had done the job they set out to do. "I think Ericsson 4 is out of reach," Bekking told reporters. "It is pretty much a fight for second now," concurred Ken Read – but what a fight. It was PUMA that struck the next blow with a brilliant in-port win to finally lift the 'bridesmaid' tag from around their necks. It cut their deficit to Telefónica Blue to just a single point. First place might have been settled, but as the race shifted gears for the final three sprint legs, a tantalising battle beckoned.

left The welcome the fleet received on arrival in Galway, late Saturday night and early Sunday morning, was one of the best. It was particularly special for the crew of Green Dragon, returning to their home port in third place after a series of poor results.

overleaf The stopover in Galway was one of the most successful the race has ever seen, with over 400,000 people visiting the Race Village to see the boats. This was the scene on the Saturday night, at a concert following the in-port racing.

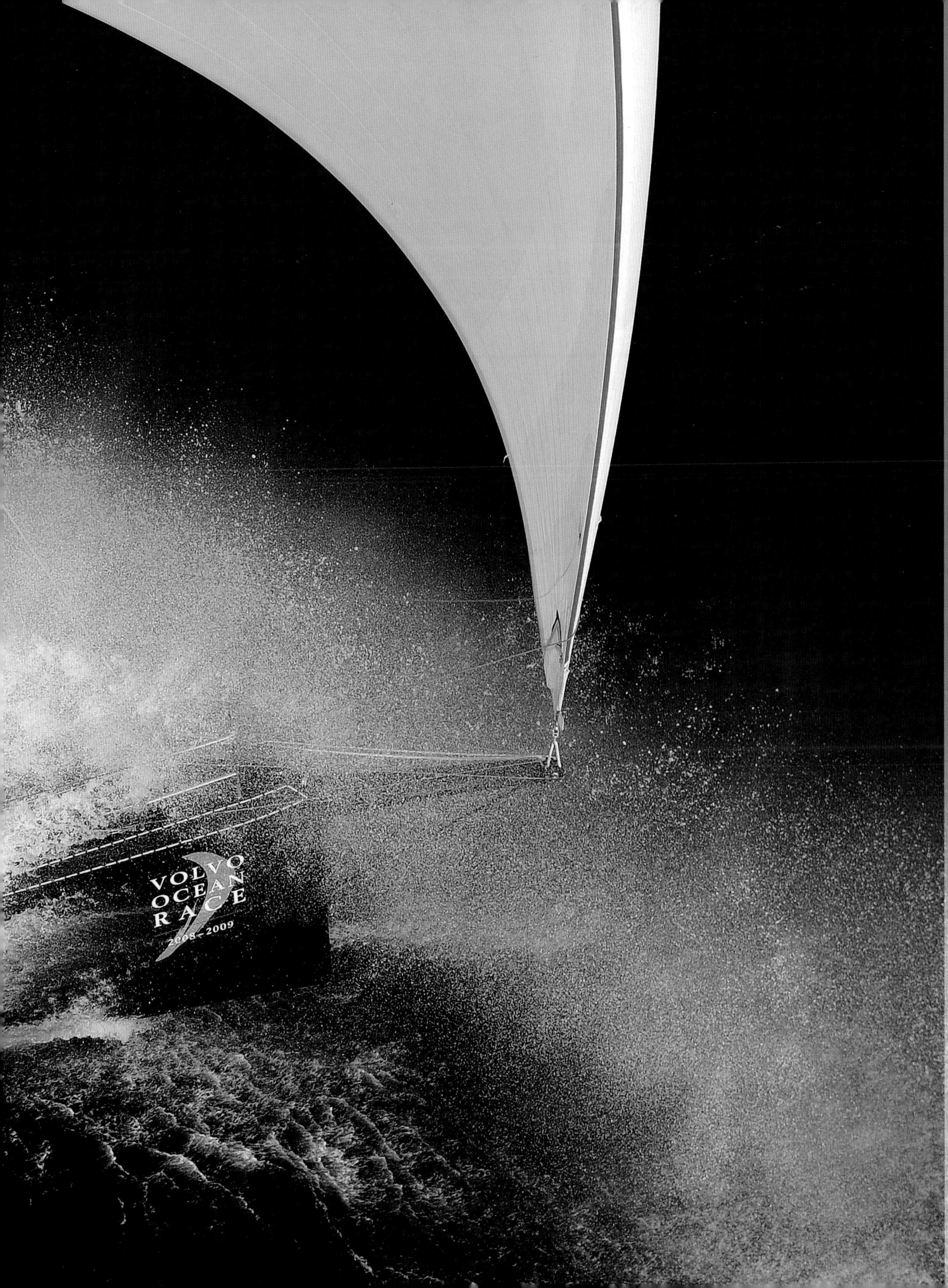

White Night

The battle for second place overall was one of contrasts. Aboard PUMA, the urbane American, Ken Read, was on his first race and up against the often outspoken Dutchman, Telefónica Blue's Bouwe Bekking, going round for the sixth time. In terms of round-the-world experience, the scales were balanced by PUMA's four-lap veteran navigator, Andrew Cape, matched against Blue's first-timer, Tom Addis. Then there were the boats: PUMA, quick in stronger breeze and second only to Ericsson 3 and 4 off the wind; and Telefónica Blue, dominant in the lighter air and upwind. So could it all just come down to the weather over the final three legs?

The 1,250 miles from Galway to Marstrand, on Sweden's west coast, opened with a short lap in front of the huge crowd that lined the harbour walls and beaches, before Ericsson 4 led Green Dragon back out into the North Atlantic. Right behind them, Telefónica Blue and PUMA were side by side. The wind increased to over 30 knots from the northeast and the fleet powered southwards down the west coast of Ireland flying their biggest masthead spinnakers – in theory, Ericsson and PUMA territory, but this time the outcome was different. From Telefónica Blue, Bouwe Bekking reported: *"The first time this race we could hang 100 per cent with the others, while running in 25–30 knots ... but we had some scary moments as well. In one squall we had 40 knots and were hanging on for dear life, we were more underwater than above. [This time] we decided to drop the big spinnaker, knowing that we would lose some distance, but keeping it in one piece was more important."*

Ericsson 4's crew decided to keep the spinnaker up, but were hit by the full force of the squall as they prepared for a gybe. They took a wave badly and spun out of control. The boat lay on its side, sails flogging and the crew unable to do anything as the ropes attached to the spinnaker almost destroyed the leeward wheel and the aluminium guard that was supposed to protect it. After a grim 30 seconds they regained control and lurched into the gybe, only to wipe out again as they completed it.

In a subsequent email, Ken Read reported, *"Last time I saw Ericsson 4, they were lying on their side blowing out to sea."* But the crew of PUMA had trouble too; having chosen the conservative option of taking the spinnaker down, it jammed. They kept the boat upright until the problem could be fixed, although for several minutes they were spearing off in the wrong direction. Meanwhile, Green Dragon still had her big spinnaker up and, at the wheel, Neal McDonald picked his moment for the gybe. A circumnavigation's worth of teamwork was distilled into a few seconds of perfect execution. Green Dragon stormed away to lead at the Fastnet Rock, completing a memorable Irish stopover for the team.

Once Ericsson 4 was up and running again, boat captain David Endean had some good news. Water had been leaking into the boat through a crack between the cockpit floor and the hull, but on the new gybe the leak had stopped, as the crack was no longer being levered open by the loads from the rig. It wasn't a structural risk, it wasn't going to get worse, and it wasn't going to slow them down. The same applied to the broken wheel; while it was smashed into eight pieces, they could use the emergency steering while they swapped the remaining, good wheel from one side to the other, each time they had to tack or gybe. Endean decided that

chapter opener **Wild conditions greeted the fleet as it left Galway and returned to the North Atlantic.**

left **Green Dragon and Delta Lloyd rip along the Cliffs of Moher, on the west coast of Ireland, with the big masthead spinnakers up. According to Green Dragon watch captain Neal McDonald, the proximity** of the coast gave the racing an inshore feel, and led to them holding on to that sail longer than they might have otherwise, as the wind increased.

right A waterspout threatens Ericsson 4. It doesn't matter whether you're in the Southern Ocean, or a few miles off the west coast of Ireland, nature always menaces. Ericsson 4's media crew, Guy Salter, wrote of this one: *"As the lines of cloud came rolling in we noticed a waterspout starting to form – these aquatic tornados are seriously bad news, but luckily it did not touch down, dissipating before our eyes."*

neither repair was critical. He could afford to wait for better conditions or a quieter moment.

It was a fast run across the Irish Sea towards the English coast, but a particularly complex weather situation was developing ahead, with small low-pressure systems moving unpredictably along the same path as the fleet, up the English Channel and into the North Sea. The first of these created a light-wind trap on the south coast of Cornwall. Green Dragon and Telefónica Black took a more southerly route to avoid it, but the trap snapped shut on the others as they rounded Lizard Point. By mid-afternoon on 7 June, Telefónica Black had gone from last to first, and was defending her lead from Green Dragon.

But to the strategists aboard Telefónica Blue, PUMA and Ericsson 4, locked in a private battle, it didn't much matter where the rest of the fleet went. Light conditions now dominated as they raced eastwards along the Channel, with everyone eventually favouring the French coast for better breeze. Green Dragon took on the notorious Alderney Race in a foul tide, her skipper, Ian Walker, writing: *"It was a highlight of the race, rock-hopping at night in fierce current, trying to steal every metre we could on the fleet."*

Meanwhile, Telefónica Black chose to go north of Alderney, only to discover, as navigator Roger Nilson wrote afterwards, that the tidal race immediately north of the island was as bad as Alderney Race: *"Suddenly we were caught in a tidal river, gybing back and forth in the 1,000-metre passage … One missed gybe and we could have been thrown up on the rocks."* It got worse when Nilson discovered that Green Dragon had passed them by creeping up the shore of the Cap de la Hague.

The pendulum quickly swung back though, and the chasing pack of Ericsson 3, Delta Lloyd, Telefónica Blue, PUMA and Ericsson 4 started to make gains by positioning themselves offshore as the sun rose on the morning of 8 June. The two leaders began to ease away from the French coast to protect their position. Aboard Telefónica Blue, Jonathan Swain had just come on deck for his watch. They were the most northerly boat, offshore and to leeward in the southerly wind, and they were apparently making rapid gains, but while they were going eastwards faster than the others, they were also slipping away to the north, and getting closer to the English coast.

It was the wrong place to be; the wind shifted to the southeast, then the east, and suddenly the fleet was sailing upwind towards the Dover Strait. Telefónica Blue suffered more of this unfavourable wind shift earlier, and then had to tack first to avoid the exclusion zone around the busy port of Dover. *"Within an hour we lost seven miles,"* Bouwe Bekking later reported in an email. Jonathan Swain finished his watch "sick to the stomach". They had not only lost touch with the whole pack, but, more importantly, with PUMA. The situation grew worse as the day progressed, and the wind became increasingly flaky as they struggled past the exclusion zone and on into the Dover Strait. By that evening, PUMA was battling with Ericsson 4 for third, while Telefónica Blue languished in last, more than 10 miles behind them.

When the wind finally steadied and picked up, it came from the northeast. Green Dragon and Telefónica Black clawed their way clear of the Dover Strait still in the lead. The northeasterly came from a new, small low-pressure system that was gathering strength and getting mobile close to the fleet. Aboard Ericsson 4, Jules Salter remembered how Pirates of the Caribbean had gone from fifth to second on the Rotterdam to Göteborg leg in 2005–06. So, once again, Salter headed for the coast to get east of the centre of low pressure.

Ericsson 4 found the southerly wind east of the low, hoisted the spinnaker in a building breeze and came screaming up the shore. The leaders realised the danger too late. Ericsson 4 passed Green Dragon and Telefónica Black at Rotterdam as they negotiated a second exclusion zone and then the Rotterdam Gate Race: a high-speed lap off the Dutch port, where a big crowd gathered to watch. The wind built strongly, and the fleet then took off north in 25 to 30 knots of southwesterly breeze, Ericsson 4 leading the way in her favourite conditions, with Green Dragon on her heels.

There were casualties; Ericsson 3 dallied offshore too long, getting caught in the light wind in the centre of the low-pressure system; they made a 45-mile loss in just six hours before they could escape. Third-placed PUMA and fourth-placed Telefónica Black both broke their front-line spinnakers off Rotterdam and drifted westwards, close to where the centre of the low still lurked. Telefónica Black's navigator, Roger Nilson, realised the danger as the wind started to drop, and they gybed back towards the Dutch coast. But PUMA carried on, until first the 13.00 GMT position report arrived with bad news, and then the light air completely engulfed them.

The mood was upbeat aboard Telefónica Blue; Ericsson 3 was behind them and now they made their first ever pass in strong breeze downwind, overtaking Delta Lloyd. But as Jonathan Swain climbed on deck for his watch on the afternoon of 9 June, he could hardly believe his ears: "PUMA is 40 miles behind and stuck in three knots of wind!" Swain and his team-mates were right back in the game.

PUMA needed a Plan B, and navigator Andrew Cape was the man to deliver. After 90 minutes of trying to escape to the east of the low's centre, Cape convinced Ken Read that their best chance was to go out to the west, where they would find a strong northerly wind. They gybed back that way, resigned to more losses, massive separation from the fleet and an upwind slog to Marstrand in 30 knots of cold breeze. "[We're] *hoping beyond hope that this new tactic works ...*" wrote Ken Read.

With second place overall slipping away from them, Andrew Cape was under the cosh as never before. That night, Rick Deppe reported: *"A tough night for all on board, cold and bumpy, while knowing that there is a huge deficit to make up creates a sombre mood, the grey sky adding the finishing touch to the misery."* But just after midnight, PUMA began to reverse her losses. Ken Read and his team were now sailing straight at the northern tip of Denmark in a solid 20 knots of northerly breeze, while everyone else was trickling up the Danish coast in an increasingly unreliable southerly wind, negotiating the centre of the low that was moving across their path.

The gap between PUMA and the rest closed again as fast as it had opened. Jonathan Swain later recalled Telefónica Blue's navigator, Tom Addis, coming on deck and starting to read the latest position report, before saying, "Something weird has gone on here ..." PUMA's gains were so big that he couldn't believe it. He returned below to reanalyse the last four position reports to see if

he could identify the problem. But the gains were real, and as Swain put it later, they were "dumbfounded" aboard Telefónica Blue.

Everything now depended on the exact movement of that capricious low pressure. Initially it went against PUMA, and the leaders of the eastern group, Ericsson 4 and Green Dragon, popped out in front of Ken Read's team at the northern tip of Denmark. These two leaders turned eastwards to where Marstrand lay across the Skagerrak. But then a rain squall arrived from the northwest. It reached PUMA first, pushing them ahead of Telefónica Blue and the rest of the eastern group. *"The guys that do this gig tend towards the non-emotional, but I tell you people are singing to themselves right now ..."* reported an incredulous Rick Deppe from PUMA as they slipped into third place.

If that wasn't bad enough for Bekking, Swain, Calafat and the rest, the squall put PUMA within chasing distance of Green Dragon. And the Dragon didn't have the pace to hold off the challenge as they raced across the Skagerrak to the finish. PUMA passed her to snatch second place behind Ericsson 4, and gain two precious points on Telefónica Blue, who was eventually fourth into Marstrand. If that wasn't a bad enough day for Team Telefónica, Delta Lloyd then sneaked past Black with some nerveless rock-dodging from navigator Wouter Verbraak. Ericsson 3 never recovered from the earlier error and finished last.

The short stopover in Marstrand was deemed a "pit-stop" by Race HQ, meaning that shore crews were not allowed to work on the boats. David Endean had found neither the conditions nor a quiet moment on the leg, and now

above **Disaster for Telefónica Blue as she runs aground while leading the fleet, just after the start of leg nine. The boat was eventually towed off the rock and returned to Marstrand for frantic repair work, to try to rejoin the fleet in Stockholm in time for the in-port racing.**

overleaf **Different kinds of wind power; Ericsson 4 is chased past the Lillgrund Wind Farm just south of the Öresund Bridge in a midsummer, high-latitude twilight. Many spectator boats intercepted the fleet as they sailed around the coast of Sweden.**

had both the wheel and the leak to repair on Ericsson 4. It took the best part of two days, and they only finished the afternoon before the start of leg nine. Their first place into Marstrand had left Endean and the rest of her crew desperately close to winning the race overall, but in the words of skipper Torben Grael they were "not there yet". And behind them, the leader board had tightened. Delta Lloyd and Green Dragon had closed on Telefónica Black and Ericsson 3 respectively, while PUMA now held a single-point advantage over Telefónica Blue. Leg nine, 525 miles around the coast of Sweden from Marstrand to Stockholm, promised to be a classic.

In a teasing wind and a difficult swell, the fleet did an opening lap in front of another enormous crowd. PUMA led away from the line and then, as the wind died and filled from a new direction, Bouwe Bekking picked a way through to the front for Telefónica Blue. But by the final mark of the lap, PUMA was right on her heels with Ericsson 3 and Green Dragon overlapped on either side. It was spectacular stuff; "Here we go, this is the match race, it's started already," was Jonathan Swain's reaction.

With PUMA just three lengths behind, Bouwe Bekking was rattling out the instructions to the crew of Telefónica Blue. They needed to set up the code zero sail for the new leg, hoist the staysail, pull up the daggerboard and get the rest of the sails stacked up on the windward side. The whole crew was in motion. Jordi Calafat was trimming the code zero and turned to reach for his jacket. A moment later he was sprawling across the deck as the boat stopped with a sickening, violent crunch.

A few seconds' silence, just a single curse in Spanish, and people picked themselves up. Then

Jonathan Swain called for the big code zero to be furled, and other urgent voices joined in as three crewmen dashed up on deck. Down below, water was pouring in through the hole torn in the hull as their daggerboard struck an isolated rock. The boat spun uncontrollably into a tack and the wind now pushed her further on, the boat forced high out of the water as it sat on the keel.

Dead astern of Blue when it happened, the stress levels on PUMA went off the gauge as the crew sought reassurance from Andrew Cape that the same wasn't about to happen to them. They dodged around the stricken boat, Read voicing his horrified reaction to the fate of Bouwe Bekking's team. With a little more time to react, third-placed Green Dragon was calmer, with skipper Ian Walker expressing a widespread concern: "I hope those guys are all right. Rocks, it's all rocks here, this whole country's made of rock."

Back on Telefónica Blue, the crew frantically tried to control the flow into the hull. The water reached the top of the generator before the emergency pumps and a desperate chain of men with buckets got it under control. And it soon became clear that they were never going to be able to free the boat on their own. The navigator was Simon Fisher, who had replaced Tom Addis for the final two sprint legs because of his greater inshore racing experience. Now, he sat down at the navigation station and picked up the satellite phone. "Oh f***, what have I done?" he whispered to himself as he dialled. He called the duty officer back at Race HQ to tell them that they were suspending racing. Free to seek help, they tried to have the boat towed backwards off the rock. The first attempt tore the tow post out of the powerboat. The second attempt tore a main winch off the deck of the yacht.

More boats arrived to watch or offer assistance, their wakes bouncing Blue on to the rock. A rudder snapped off – a blessing, otherwise it might have been pushed up through the hull and ripped another hole. Then PUMA's support boat joined them, with Neil Cox, Sean Healey, Will Oxley and Kimo Worthington aboard. Now the crew of Telefónica Blue had people who understood the boat, spoke the language and had the equipment. And eventually, with one tow rope attached to the base of the mast and another heeling the yacht over by pulling from the top of the rig, they got her off. Those four PUMA men later won the Wallenius Wilhelmsen Logistics Seamanship Award, for both the leg and overall. It was a long quiet tow back to Marstrand. As the reality struck home, Jonathan Swain described mixed emotions: anger, disappointment, and a part of him that simply didn't care any more. At one point he wondered where his passport was, determined just to walk off when they got to the dock. He didn't, and later, in a more reflective mood, he said, "If we were one metre to the right we would have missed the rock. Or, had we decided to pull the daggerboard up before we put the staysail up, or pulled the daggerboard up before we decided to finish the stack, we wouldn't have even known that rock was there."

Dockside back in Marstrand, Bekking was as blunt as ever: "It is clearly our own mistake, of course; we thought we were to leeward [of the rock] and clear of it and we smacked it right on the head." But Bekking knew who was taking it hardest. "The saddest person is SiFi [Simon Fisher]," he said. "I don't know how many thousand times he has said sorry." Fisher explained that he had given Bekking a course to steer past the rock, and then turned to help with the sails. He said: "I thought I had given the right numbers to be clear of the rock, but I hadn't. I thought we would be clear by a few metres, but we weren't. I've been over what happened in my head so many times, over the mistake. It's just the most awful feeling, devastating. It was just horrible."

Leading south through the Öresund Sound in the strong westerly breeze, PUMA looked to have the overall second place under lock and key. The spinnakers were hoisted as they cleared the southwest corner of Sweden, and the course eased eastwards around the country's southern tip. Inevitably, Ericsson 4 moved up to challenge in the fast downwind conditions. Then the breeze dropped a little as they turned back north and came under the influence of the east coast, and Ken Read and Andrew Cape took PUMA too close to the beach. The fleet closed and Ericsson 3 joined the leading pair as the westerly returned in strength.

It was now a three-way battle, a boat-speed race north, tinged with the concern that lighter winds were forecast before they finished. They hit a change in conditions in the early afternoon, just as the leaders were clearing the island of Öland. From PUMA, Ken Read wrote, *"Reaching along at 15 knots and then bang, upwind in five knots. Where did that come from?"* The westerly wind evaporated, replaced by a light northeasterly. But aboard Ericsson 3, media crew Gustav Morin reckoned, *"It did not come as a surprise though, Aksel [Magdahl, navigator] was more or less waiting for it to happen."* Ericsson 3 crept around the leaders, but there was another turnover coming – the old westerly breeze filled back in, and PUMA was on that side. Ken

left **Telefónica Black charges downwind; notice how the radar on the front of the mast keeps itself level with the water.**

Read's team picked up speed first, and just got across in front of Ericsson 3 before the new wind fully reached the Nordic crew. The pair accelerated northwards, leaving Ericsson 4 behind. For once, Torben Grael and Jules Salter were out of position, too far to the east, and they dropped to third.

The straight-line drag race resumed in conditions where Ericsson 3 had a tiny speed edge. But a Volvo Open 70 makes a big hole in the air and the water, and the team aboard PUMA was using that aero and hydrodynamic swirl to make life as tough as possible for the pursuing Nordics. PUMA reached the lighthouse at Almagrundet with a narrow lead, and turned west to sail the final miles to the finish at the island of Sandhamn. Now Ericsson 3 made her move. The crew had spotted a rain cloud to the south and prepared a new sail out of sight. They changed to it as they rounded the lighthouse, tacking away from PUMA.

Read and his team were caught napping, and for three or four minutes it was frenzied action as they prepared a sail to respond. But by the time they went after Ericsson 3 there was more wind on the south side of the racetrack, and as the two boats came back together the Nordics blasted into the lead. On PUMA, as Rick Deppe remembered afterwards, he heard Ken Read muttering, "I've got it," as he stepped up to take the wheel. And when they turned on to the home straight, he started tacking PUMA over and over again.

Boat-on-boat was Ken Read's game, with three America's Cup campaigns on his CV before he had turned to the Volvo Ocean Race. His experienced and super-slick crew piled on the pressure and finally forced an error. Ericsson 3's headsail got hung up on the radar

dome on the front of the mast. The boat sat head to wind, sails flogging, speed peeling off as Martin Krite free-climbed the rig to release it. It was a painful moment for the young Nordic team and their veteran skipper. It was the same mistake that they had made at the start in Cape Town. Then it had barely mattered, but now, as they watched PUMA sail past to take the gun, it cost them victory into their home port. But for Ken Read and his PUMA crew it was the sweetest moment of all: finally, a leg win.

After all that drama, the fleet filed into Sandhamn in an order that gave the leader board an anticlimactic air of finality. Ericsson 4 took third, which made it mathematically certain that they were the overall winners. Telefónica Black came home fourth, with Green Dragon and Delta Lloyd fifth and sixth. There were still 12 points available to the winner of both the Stockholm in-port racing and leg 10. But with the closest gap on the overall leader board being PUMA's seven-point advantage over Telefónica Blue, no one was expecting the order to change: Ericsson 4, PUMA, Telefónica Blue, Ericsson 3, Green Dragon, Telefónica Black, Delta Lloyd and Team Russia would be how it ended.

The Telefónica Blue team made an all-out attempt to keep their hopes alive. With help from the other shore crews, the people of Marstrand and a superhuman effort on the part of their boatbuilders, they resumed racing on the evening of 17 June. It was just three and a half days after the grounding, and they finished in Stockholm a little under two days later. But it still left them with less than two days to rest and prepare for the in-port racing, where they had to beat PUMA, or

above **Telefónica Black and PUMA** duel for the final-leg victory into St Petersburg in the golden light of a white night. Unlike Ericsson 3 at the end of leg nine, skipper (and Olympic gold medallist) Fernando Echávarri and his crew kept their nerve and held off PUMA.

overleaf **Team Russia** accompanied the fleet to St Petersburg, and led the parade along the River Neva and into the heart of the city. They moored up at the Peter and Paul Fortress in front of huge crowds for a spectacular end to the Volvo Ocean Race 2008–09.

concede second overall. So when Telefónica Blue rounded the first mark of the first Stockholm in-port race in last place, it would have been easy for their heads to go down. Instead, they spotted a wind shift, split from the fleet and passed three boats on the second leg, overtaking one more on the final lap to finish third.

In front of a countless armada of spectator boats, Telefónica Blue sailed a much better opening leg in the second race. They led at the first mark; then, as they had done so many times, sailed away from the fleet. Bouwe Bekking and his team added the overall in-port series prize to their long list of achievements with their fourth win. But, crucially, PUMA was second, which left the gap at 6.5 points. There were still eight points available for the winner of leg 10, but the scoring system awarded two points to any boat that started the final leg. Only another rock or an act of God could stop Ken Read and his team, and there was to be no final, extraordinary twist in the tale. Once PUMA had crossed the start line, leg 10 to St Petersburg was effectively a coronation parade for Ericsson 4 – which didn't stop the crews looking for that final win.

And it was PUMA again who took the early lead as they headed across the Baltic towards the Gulf of Finland, to where St Petersburg lay 400 miles away at the eastern end. Team Russia had reappeared with a new crew, and were sailing home as a non-combatant. The forecast was for the solid breeze to be replaced by lighter air from the same northeast direction, so the racetrack would be dominated by upwind sailing; conditions that the Telefónica boats loved. In those conditions, Telefónica Black had often led the fleet, only

for their challenge to unravel with the arrival of breezy downwind sailing. This time that transition was unlikely, and the skipper of Telefónica Black, Fernando Echávarri, had taken the decision to leave behind as much gear as possible, including four sails, in an all-out effort to optimise their performance for the anticipated conditions.

It was a strategy that had famously worked for Knut Frostad and djuice to win the final leg in 2001–02, when Frostad had left behind three crewmen to reduce weight. When the fleet set off into a 15 to 20-knot northeasterly breeze, Telefónica Black's plan looked decidedly risky. But once in the Gulf of Finland, the wind started to fade and Telefónica Black, along with PUMA and Ericsson 3, realised big gains on the Finnish coast. It came down to Telefónica Black versus PUMA as they closed on St Petersburg, and the crew of Black needed cool heads as they first passed, and then tried to hold Ken Read's team at bay. But as Roger Nilson said afterwards, "Suddenly it was easy to understand why Fernando won an Olympic gold last summer!" After a 21-tack duel with PUMA in the final miles of a glorious white night, Telefónica Black took her first win, and the Volvo Ocean Race 2008–09 was over.

Endgame

The fleet paraded into the heart of St Petersburg on the afternoon of 27 June, motoring up the River Neva under historic bridges, accompanied by fireworks, brass bands and crowds packed on to the embankments. There was a final round of press conferences and prize-givings, and at the finale, a bottle of vodka on every table ensured that it all finished with some of the flavour of the wild old days of the early Whitbread races. The one moment that everyone could remember the following morning was Petra van Rij's speech, as she presented PUMA's Michi Müeller with the new Hans Horrevoets Rookie Award, in memory of her late husband's work to bring young people into the top flight of ocean racing:

"My life completely changed on 18 May 2006. And although since 18 May 2006 not a single day is natural, and although since 18 May 2006 every day is an exceptional day, today is particularly exceptional.

"Exceptional, because even today I am still living my life, together with our two beautiful little girls. Exceptional, because you all finished this race healthy and in one piece. Exceptional, because today the first Hans Horrevoets Rookie Trophy will be presented.

"Hans was always pushing young sailors to reach their full potential. This trophy in his memory will keep alive his spirit. And even though I wish not to be on this spot today, I am seized with emotion knowing that Hans is remembered, knowing he will not be forgotten. I wish to congratulate you with a trophy I never wanted to present, and wish you all the best in your beautiful sailing career. Congratulations and be safe."

It was a time for both looking forward and looking back, with some stories ending as others started, and everyone scattering to the four corners of the planet. Ericsson 4 never got the right conditions to have another go at the 24-hour record, so the 600-mile barrier remains intact. Oleg Zherebtsov tied Team Russia up in front of the Peter and Paul Fortress, just as he had hoped, but Jeremy Elliott remained at home designing sails, and married Jo at the end of August. Roger Nilson had done six races, and was planning that this should be the last. "I hope no one asks me, and if they do I hope I have the courage to say no," he said. The addictive element in his personality, which might undermine that plan, would continue to influence his life. He was intending to do a film about it, and continue training to be a therapist for people with addictive disorders.

Improbable as it may sound, many of the sailors were off to start new sailboat races in the days that followed. David Endean and Stu Bannatyne would both compete in the Transpacific Yacht Race from Los Angeles to Hawaii, claiming that it was "on the way home" to New Zealand, although neither was planning more than a few weeks with their families afterwards. Jonathan Swain and Jules Salter would be sailing the Fastnet Race together, with Swain competing against Telefónica team-mate Jordi Calafat, who would be there on a different boat.

Many were going home to put in some proper time as husbands and fathers. Jerry Kirby would return to the States to support his wife Kim in her battle against cancer. Tom Braidwood felt that the race's schedule had made it impossible for him to maintain his family relationships, and returned to Australia to do just that. Neal McDonald was planning a summer and autumn of childcare, as his wife Lisa was expecting their second baby at the end of August. The pieces of his cut-off wedding ring had found their way into Lisa's safer hands, but not yet to a jeweller for repair. Martin Krite was anxious to give his wife Emilie the freedom to return to her work as a doctor, so he was not going back to his theology course immediately, as it would have meant Emilie making further sacrifices. "It's not the highest priority right now," he said, "it's just family that are the most important."

Rick Deppe planned to return with his family to Ireland for the summer, and work on developing his own documentary about the fishing industry. Gerd-Jan Poortman and Neil Cox would stay with their boats for a while, the former sailing Delta Lloyd back to Holland, where he would skipper her for three months of corporate sailing for the sponsor. Cox would sail PUMA to Stockholm for decommissioning, and then take a holiday at a location "undisclosed even to myself".

Everyone took something away from the race; for Jordi Calafat part of the joy was the roller-coaster ride of Telefónica Blue ("You learn a lot from the downs"), but he was happiest to have left Alicante with 10 friends and finished in St Petersburg still with 10 friends. Martin Krite made the same point about making lasting friendships. But he also remembered moments like the one when 30 killer whales had surfaced near the boat on the way to Qingdao, when only he and Magnus Olsson were on deck, and he had just felt lucky to be out there.

For Neal McDonald, one of the best moments had been the spectacular gybe off the Irish coast that had allowed Green Dragon to lead away from her homeland.

Rick Deppe left with the overall Inmarsat Media Prize, and the realisation that the race had been as tough in this new role, and meant as much to him, as the first time he had done it as a rookie bowman. Jerry Kirby had been round the world twice with Deppe, and for him it had been the hardest race, but not because of what had happened on the water. With Kim's illness and the economy in turmoil, PUMA had become a refuge, the boat a "safe, happy place". He now understood that "life at the extreme was a privilege and not a right".

For Gerd-Jan Poortman there was the disappointment of missing Cape Horn for the second race in succession, but he reckoned that he would "hopefully [be] coming back to tick that off". The best and most vivid memories for Neil Cox stemmed from the stopover in India: completing on schedule the repair of the damage that PUMA had sustained during leg two in 40 °C (104 °F) heat, against a background of mosques, elephants, and thousands of people queuing for the Race Village attractions.

Others emphasised lessons that they would take on to future projects. Tom Braidwood understood that their boat-speed problems had come "as a direct result of decisions made before the first layer of carbon hit the mould. Other teams were able to pull from experience gained from the last event. We did not have the time or the dollars to do that." Jonathan Swain was relieved that they had finally learned to sail their boat downwind in strong breeze – if only they had figured it out before the start!

The winners put the same emphasis on preparation; Stu Bannatyne repeated over and over that it had taken a total team effort, across every area, from the sailors to the cooks. Even the families: "A happy wife means a productive sailor," he said, "and Ericsson has looked after them really well." Asked to pick a best and worst moment from his second race win, David Endean couldn't, saying, "It's just a blur." And for Jules Salter: "I've wanted to do the race since being a five- or six-year-old and watching the boats finish in Portsmouth. To win has been an ambition since I was 13 or 14 and I was reading a book by someone who is helping me in this race right now, Mike Quilter. I feel extremely happy."

But what of the skipper of the winning boat, Torben Grael? He had largely kept his counsel – interviews in English, however fluent, were nevertheless in a second language. He wrote emails from the boat only a handful of times, was rarely interviewed while sailing, and gave almost nothing away. After the race was over he admitted that media attention was not his "favourite part of the job"; in his view "it's a distraction". A distraction from the focus that had allowed him to win five Olympic medals, six World Championships, a Louis Vuitton Cup and now the Volvo Ocean Race.

Clues to his temperament came from his team-mates. Asked by Guy Salter who might play their skipper in the Hollywood movie of the adventure, the favoured choices were Antonio Banderas or John McEnroe. But it was Grael's desire to win that shone through most clearly over the long months of challenge. It was there in the unguarded moments at the end of the toughest stages, the exhaustion clear in his face, but the eyes still burning.

And there was one telling moment in Singapore, in front of the International Jury that oversaw the event's rule compliance. No one felt that Ericsson 4's possible infringement, concerning a bow repair, was anything more than a technicality, an administrative oversight. Nevertheless, rules are rules, and if the hearing were to go against them, it had the potential to reduce Ericsson 4's points total at the end of leg three to zero. It could destroy the team's chance of the overall prize.

Grael was faced with an impossible situation that almost certainly (given the divided responsibilities in the big teams) wasn't of his making, but for which he could pay a very heavy price. And it quickly became clear just how much he wanted to win the race when he spoke to the jury, his voice breaking, the emotion thick in every word:

"I am almost 50 years old and I have dedicated my entire life to sailing. I can hold the pressure ... I can hold the pressure of being the tactician of an Italian America's Cup team in two Louis Vuitton finals, and I can hold the pressure of sailing six Olympic Games. I can hold the pressure of sailing 600 miles in 24 hours, but I cannot hold the pressure of this ..."

Grael left the room. The jury found for Ericsson 4. And the rest, as they say, is history.

Volvo Open 70

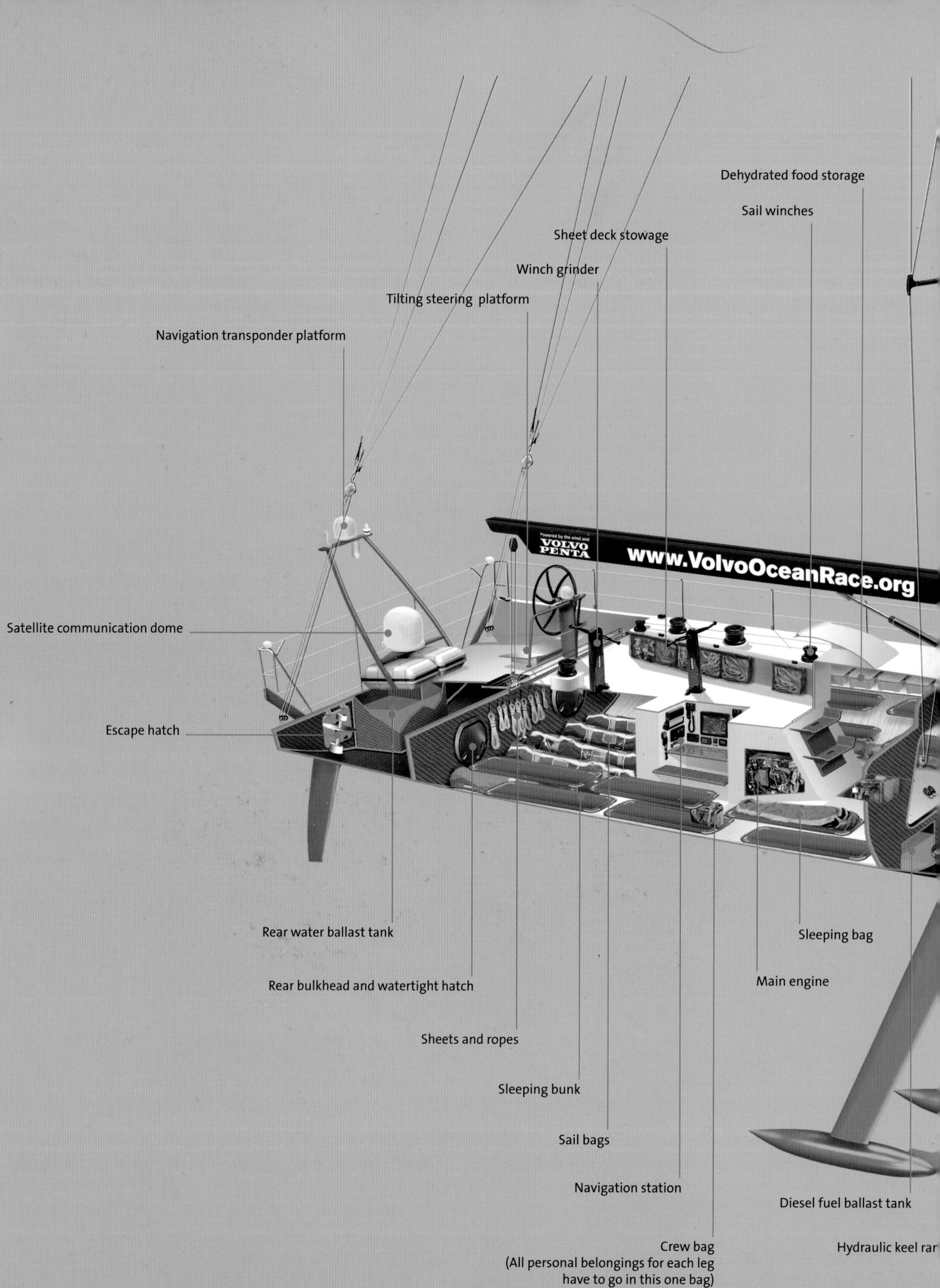
Dehydrated food storage
Sail winches
Sheet deck stowage
Winch grinder
Tilting steering platform
Navigation transponder platform
Satellite communication dome
Escape hatch
Powered by the wind and
VOLVO
PENTA
www.VolvoOceanRace.org
Rear water ballast tank
Rear bulkhead and watertight hatch
Sheets and ropes
Sleeping bunk
Sail bags
Navigation station
Crew bag
(All personal belongings for each leg
have to go in this one bag)
Sleeping bag
Main engine
Diesel fuel ballast tank
Hydraulic keel rar

Retractable daggerboard

Galley

Toilet

Sink

Foredeck hatch

VOLVO
OCEAN
RACE
ROUND THE WORLD

Bowsprit

Watertight hatch

Watertight bulkhead

Swing keel

Top of swing keel

Glossary

Abandon ship: To leave a fatally distressed vessel. An abandon-ship bag (grab-bag) is a container of emergency and survival gear pre-prepared by the crew to take with them if they have to abandon ship, usually containing tools, water, VHF radio, flares, food, etc.

Aft: Towards or at the back of the boat.

Apparent wind: The wind that blows over the boat modified by the boat's forward progress. The wind direction felt on the boat as it moves, a combination of the true wind blowing over the land, and the wind created by the boat's movement relative to the land.

Astern: Behind the boat.

Asymmetric spinnaker: A downwind sail, flown from the bow of a boat, often from a short bowsprit. Sometimes called A-sail and, incorrectly, gennaker. Asymmetric spinnakers can only be flown one way round, i.e. with one dedicated corner, the tack, attached to the spinnaker pole or the bowsprit; one dedicated corner, the head, attached to the halyard; and one dedicated corner, the clew, attached to a sheet.

Back: Pull a sail against the wind so that it fills on the wrong side. Also to force the boat to sail backwards – back down – by pushing the sails back against the wind so that weed or other debris may be washed off the keel or rudder.

Backstay: The stay linking the top of the mast and the stern.

Batten: Thin strip of composite material inserted into a pocket in a sail to support the sail's shape.

Beam: The width of the boat at the widest point. Also the side of the boat (e.g. 'wind on the beam' means the wind is coming sideways on to the boat).

Beat: Sail a zigzag course to make progress into the wind, as it is impossible for a boat to sail directly into the wind.

Block: A pulley used for changing the direction of a line or in making up a simple system to multiply the force applied to a line.

Boat captain: There is an important distinction between the racing skipper of a Volvo Open 70 and the boat captain. While the former is in charge of the yacht out on the water, the boat captain is responsible for all the maintenance and preparation of the yacht both ashore and at sea.

Boom: The spar (rigid pole) at the bottom edge of a sail, generally the mainsail.

Bow: The front of the boat.

Bowman: The crew member who is responsible for most things that happen forward of the mast. Rigs the gear for spinnakers and for headsail changes, is usually the one whisked up the rig if anything goes wrong. Most often seen wearing a climbing harness over all his sailing gear and carrying strapped thereto rolls of tape, spikes, knives, karabiners, snap shackles, sail ties, etc.

Bowsprit: A projecting spar extending from the bow of a boat, generally used in the modern era to fly an asymmetric spinnaker. Volvo Open 70s have 1.82m-long carbon-fibre bowsprits on which to fly their A-sails.

Broach: An uncontrolled, sudden alteration of course usually when sailing fast downwind.

Broad reach: When the wind is between 90 and 130 degrees off the bow.

Bulb: A torpedo-shaped construction fastened at the bottom of the keel foil.

Bulkhead: A vertical panel or partition, often with a dual purpose in a Volvo Open 70: it is part of the yacht's structure and forms a watertight compartment in case the hull is breached.

Buoy: A floating object anchored to the bottom of the sea. Some are for navigation, some are for mooring to, others are set temporarily to mark out a race course.

Canting keel: A canting keel is hinged at the bottom of the hull and canted from side to side by massive hydraulic rams. This enables the crew to swing the ballast bulb to the windward side to counteract the forces of the sails trying to heel the boat over.

Carbon: Strong and stable material used in the hull, rudders and daggerboards.

Chainplates: The attachments for shrouds and stays; part of the hull that connects the hull to the rig.

Close reach: When the wind is between 50 and 90 degrees off the bow.

Cockpit: The lowered portion of the deck aft of the mast, where the crew stands to work.

Code zero: A sail for light air with the maximum possible surface area, attached to the end of the bowsprit, the top of the mast, and right in the stern of the boat.

Daggerboard: A retractable keel, a hydrodynamically shaped plate that slides up and down through a watertight casing in the hull. Volvo Open 70s have two daggerboards forward of the mast which supply lateral resistance to stop the boat slipping sideways under the force of the sails, when the canting keel is swung out to the side to keep the boat upright.

Doldrums: An area around the equator which has little wind, and lots of squalls and rain showers.

Endoscope: A device inserted through the hull just ahead of the rudders or keel, so that the leading edge can be inspected for any snagged material – weed or pieces of fishing net. Any debris that isn't too big can be swept off the keel by a 'flossing' rope, usually a piece of rope attached to the end of a long rod that can be swept down the leading edge of the keel or rudder.

Foredeck: The deck in front of the mast.

Forestay: The wire, rod or synthetic stay at the front of the boat used to hold up the mast. Sometimes there is more than one forestay.

Foul-weather gear: Waterproof clothing worn to protect the user from as much of the spray and waves bursting over the boat as possible.

Freeze-dried food: Lightweight food carried aboard long-distance racing boats. The food is reconstituted by pouring boiling water into the pack, stirring well and then allowing it to stand until it absorbs the water.

Front: A weather front is a line representing the transition between two air masses; an air mass is a section of the earth's atmosphere which has relatively uniform temperature and moisture, but not uniform pressure. Fronts generally cause changes in wind speed and direction as they pass.

Galley: The kitchen on board.

Gennaker: A cross between a spinnaker and genoa, used for broad reaching.

GPS: Global Positioning System: a satellite navigation system that fixes a position on the earth's surface by comparing the minute time differences between signals transmitted from a selection of satellites and a controlling ground station. For the Volvo Ocean Race, navigators have to carry sextants and know how to use them in order to use conventional sun- or star-sight navigation if there is a catastrophic breakdown of GPS, either on the boat or in the system itself.

Grinder: A crew member who is using the pedestal system in the cockpit to apply force to the winches. Also the winch system itself, which is operated through the pedestal system – the grinder pedestal.

Gybe: Change direction by turning so that the stern of the boat passes through the wind. This means that the sails, particularly the mainsail, can swing across with great force; gybing has to be approached with care.

Halyard: A rope used to hoist a sail.

Harness: A webbing harness worn about the torso, generally over any clothing, with a detachable tether made from nylon with attachment hooks. Intended to prevent a crew member from falling overboard and becoming separated from the boat.

Headsail: One of the triangular sails set forward of the mast; the word is interchangeable with 'jib'.

Heel: A boat heels when it leans over due to the sideways force of the wind.

Helm: Not the person who steers the boat – that is the helmsman or helmswoman – but the device with which they steer, either a tiller or a wheel.

Helmsman/woman: The person steering the boat.

In-port racing: Between the 10 legs that are raced from one stopover port to the next, there are other point-scoring opportunities that count towards the overall leader board. The in-port racing is one of these, and in the Volvo Ocean Race 2008–09 it consisted of two short races during a single day. The two race scores were combined to get a result for the day, and the winner then received 4.0 points towards the overall leader board, second place got 3.5, third place 3.0 points, and so on.

Instruments: Sailing instruments aboard a Volvo Open 70 show on various displays a vast amount of information, such as true and apparent wind speed and direction, velocity made good (VMG), course made good (CMG), boat speed, depth, water temperature, and data from the GPS navigation system.

Jackstay: A wire or length of webbing secured on the deck of the yacht to which safety harnesses can be attached.

Jib: A triangular sail set in front of the mast.

Keel: The wing-shaped steel foil that is mounted under the middle of the boat, enabling the boat to be sailed against the wind and preventing drift and capsize.

Knot: A measurement of speed based on the time it takes to cover one nautical mile. A yacht travelling at one knot is sailing one nautical mile per hour.

Latitude: Imaginary lines running parallel east to west around the globe. They help you to measure position and distance on a chart when used in conjunction with lines of longitude.

Leeward: Direction that the wind blows towards; i.e. with your back to the wind, you will be looking to leeward.

Leeway: Sideways drift caused by the wind.

Leverage: See Separation.

Lifejacket: Will keep a person fully afloat with their head clear of the water even if unconscious, unlike a buoyancy aid. Usually an inflatable device, sometimes with automatic gas inflation.

Longitude: Imaginary lines running around the globe north to south, which divide the world like segments of an orange. Used with lines of latitude to measure position and distance.

Mainsail: The large sail attached to the back of the mast.

Mast: The spar on which the sails are hoisted. On Volvo Open 70s, made from carbon fibre.

Masthead sail: Sails that are hoisted to the top of the mast.

Mastman: The crewmember who is responsible for helping the bowman to hoist and drop sails.

Match racing: A racing format where only two yachts compete at a time, like a boxing match, as opposed to fleet racing, where more yachts sail at once. Occasionally, when the situation demands it, two yachts may pair up to match race each other in a fleet race.

Nautical mile: A distance unit at sea, equivalent to a minute of latitude measured at the equator: 1,852 m (6,075 ft).

Navigator: The crew member who spends most of the time assessing all the factors which combine to direct the boat along the fastest course to the finish.

Pedestal: A structure in the cockpit that is linked to the winch system via shafts below the cockpit floor. It has waist-height rotary handles that allow the crew to apply power to the winches. The system usually includes gearboxes that can be clutched to any of the main winch drums, so maximum crew power can be applied to any sheet or halyard via the pedestals.

Pitman: The crew member responsible for the halyards and some other sail-shaping controls.

Port: The left-hand side of the boat (facing forwards).

Port tack or gybe: Sailing with the wind blowing over the port side of the boat.

Position report: A report on every boat's position, sent by Volvo Ocean Race Headquarters.

Radar: An electronic instrument that shows ice, ships, rain, or land near the boat. The radar sends out signals whose returning echo is then registered and measured.

Reach: Sail with the wind on the side of the boat.

Reef: Make the sails smaller in strong winds.

Rig: Catch-all term for the mast and boom, sails, and standing and running rigging: the motor powerhouse of the boat.

Rigging: The rods, wires or composite stays used to support the mast (standing rigging) and the ropes used to control the sails, etc, as well as moveable stays holding up the mast, like the running backstays (running rigging).

Rudder: A hydrodynamically shaped vertical foil sticking down into the water, it can be turned from side to side to steer the boat.

Rudder stock: The vertical shaft that holds the rudder in the boat. It turns on bearings and transfers the steering effort from the wheels, via the quadrant, to the rudder blade in the water. Stocks on Volvo Open 70s are usually made from carbon fibre.

Run: Sail with the wind behind you.

Running rigging: All the ropes used for raising, lowering and controlling the sails.

Safety line: Webbing strap about 1.5m long with snap hooks. Fastened to the personal safety harness and the boat.

Sail loft: A place where sails are made and repaired.

Scoring gate: In addition to the points awarded for winning the legs, there were further opportunities to gain points at the scoring gates. These were set at various places on the longer legs, and the points added to the overall leader board. The winner received 4.0 points, second place got 3.5, third place 3.0 points, and so on.

Separation (or leverage): The distance between the boats measured at 90 degrees to a line running from the start to finish of the race course.

Sheet: A rope that controls a sail.

Skipper: The person in charge on board.

Southern Ocean: Used to refer to the oceans between Antarctica and around 40 deg S.

Spinnaker: A big, lightweight sail for faster sailing off the wind. There are asymmetric and symmetrical spinnakers; Volvo Open 70s use only asymmetric spinnakers.

Stanchions: The posts which hold lifelines along the rail.

Starboard: The right-hand side of the boat (facing forwards).

Starboard tack or gybe: Sailing with the wind blowing over the starboard side of the boat.

Staysail: A small headsail set back from the bow and between the jib and mainsail to effectively narrow the slot between the jib and the mainsail. Also used when sailing at certain wind angles with an asymmetrical spinnaker.

StealthPlay: A StealthPlay allows the skipper of a race yacht to hide its position from the rest of the fleet and the world for a predetermined period. Once the yacht calls in a StealthPlay to Race HQ, all the yacht's position-report data is removed from the public domain for the next 12 or 24 hours, depending on the leg.

Stern: The back of the boat.

Storm jib: A very small headsail fastened on the forestay and used in strong winds or bad waves.

Strobe: A small emergency light, which gives off sharp blinks. Everyone carries one at night in case they fall overboard.

Tack: Change direction by turning the bow of the boat through the wind. Also the bottom forward corner of a sail.

Tiller: A horizontal rod, bar or similar device attached to the top of the rudder and used to steer the boat.

Trade winds: The stable, strong winds which blow both sides of the Doldrums.

Transom: The flat section across the back – or stern – of the boat.

Trim: Keeps the boat level fore and aft.

Trimmer: The crew member with special responsibility for adjusting the sails to every nuance of wind speed or direction.

True wind: The direction and strength of the wind when the boat is dead in the water. When under way, instruments calculate the true wind by taking into account boat speed and apparent wind.

Trysail: An emergency sail for very severe wind conditions. It is made from heavyweight synthetic sailcloth, usually set without a boom and often tied round the mast so it can be used if there has been a major failure of the mainsail or mast.

Upwind: A term often used instead of 'beat', as in 'to beat' is 'to sail upwind', but also used to describe a place that's closer to the direction the wind is coming from than the speaker, e.g. 'that island is two miles upwind'.

Watch: One part of a crew that has been divided so that some may sleep while others race the boat. A watch is also the period of time that the crew spends operating the boat.

Watch captain: The crew member who is in charge of that particular watch, usually a very experienced crew who has sailed the race before. Deputises for the skipper when he is off-watch and tends to lead the watch in boat handling when the skipper and/or navigator is occupied with tactical planning.

Whitbread 60: The class name of the boats participating in the 1993–94 and 1997–98 Whitbread Round the World Races, and the Volvo Ocean Race 2001–02, for which it was named the Volvo Ocean 60.

Winch: A mechanical device for tensioning lines, for instance a jib sheet. The drum of a winch is turned by gearing, using either a handle inserted in the top, or via a grinder pedestal which can be connected to a number of different winches on the boat.

Windward: Direction that the wind blows from; i.e. with your face to the wind, you will be looking to windward.

Volvo Ocean Race History

RACE ONE 1973–74

1.	Sayula II	Mexico	Ramón Carlin	
2.	Adventure	UK	Patrick Bryans	
			Malcom Skene	
			George Vallings	
			Roy Mullender	
3.	Grand Louis	France	André Viant	
4.	Kriter	France	Jack Grout	
			Michel Malinovsky	
			Alain Gliksman	
5.	Guia	Italy	Giorgio Falck	
6.	Great Britain II	UK	Chay Blyth	
7.	Second Life	UK	Roddy Ainslie	
8.	Cserb	Italy	Doi Malingri	
9.	British Soldier	UK	James Myatt	
10.	Tauranga	Italy	Eric Pascoli	
11.	Copernicus	Poland	Zygfryd Perlicki	
12.	33 Export	France	Jean-Pierre Millet	
			Dominique Guillet	
13.	Otago	Poland	Zdzisław Pieńkawa	
14.	Peter von Danzig	Germany	Reinhard Laucht	

Pen Duick VI	France	Eric Tabarly	DNF
Burton Cutter	UK	Leslie Williams	
		Alan Smith	DNF
Jakaranda	South Africa	John Goodwin	DNF
Concorde	France	Pierre Chassin	DNF
Pen Duick III	France	M Cuiklinksi	DNF

THE ROUTE		DISTANCE 27,000 NM
Leg 1	Portsmouth to Cape Town	Start 8 Sep 1973
Leg 2	Cape Town to Sydney	Restart 7 Nov 1973
Leg 3	Sydney to Rio de Janeiro	Restart 29 Dec 1973
Leg 4	Rio de Janeiro to Portsmouth	Restart 6 March 1974

RACE TWO 1977–78

1.	Flyer	Netherlands	Cornelis van Rietschoten
2.	King's Legend	UK	Nick Radcliff
			Mike Clancy
3.	Traité de Rome	EEC	Philippe Hanin
4.	Disque d'Or	Switzerland	Pierre Fehlmann
5.	ADC Accutrac	UK	Clare Francis
6.	Gauloises II	France	Eric Loizeau
7.	Adventure	UK	James Watts
			David Leslie
			Ian Bailey-Willmot
			Robin Duchesne
8.	Neptune	France	Bernard Deguy
9.	B & B Italia	Italy	Corrado di Majo
10.	33 Export	France	Alain Gabbay
11.	Tielsa	Netherlands	Dirk Nauta
12.	Great Britain II	UK	Rob James
13.	Debenhams	UK	John Ridgway
14.	Japy-Hermès	France	Jean-Michel Viant
15.	Heath's Condor	UK	Leslie Williams
			Robin Knox Johnston

THE ROUTE		DISTANCE 26,780 NM
Leg 1	Portsmouth to Cape Town	Start 27 Aug 1977
Leg 2	Cape Town to Auckland	Restart 25 Oct 1977
Leg 3	Auckland to Rio de Janeiro	Restart 26 Dec 1977
Leg 4	Rio de Janeiro to Portsmouth	Restart 22 Feb 1978

RACE THREE 1981–82

1.	Flyer	Netherlands	Cornelis van Rietschoten
2.	Charles Heidsieck III	France	Alain Gabbay
3.	Kriter XI	France	André Viant
4.	Disque d'Or III	Switzerland	Pierre Fehlmann
5.	Outward Bound	New Zealand	Digby Taylor
6.	Xargo III	South Africa	Padda Kuttel
7.	Mor bihan	France	Philippe Poupon
8.	Berge Viking	Norway	Peder Lunde
9.	Alaska Eagle	USA	Skip Novak
			Neil Bergt
10.	Euromarché	France	Eric Tabarly
11.	Ceramco New Zealand	New Zealand	Peter Blake
12.	Skopbank of Finland	Finland	Kenneth Gahmberg
13.	RollyGo	Italy	Giorgio Falck
14.	Traité de Rome	EEC	Antonio Chioatto
15.	Croky	Belgium	Gustaaf Versluys
16.	FCF Challenger	UK	Leslie Williams
17.	United Friendly	UK	Chay Blyth
18.	Walross III Berlin	Germany	Jean-Michel Viant
19.	Licor 43	Spain	Joaquin Coello
20.	Ilgagomma	Italy	Roberto Vianello

European Uni. Belgium	Belgium	Jean Blondiau	DNF
33 Export	France	Phillipe Schaff	DNF
Gauloises III	France	Eric Loizeau	DNF
La Barca Laboratorio	Italy	Claudio Stampi	DNF
Save Venice	Italy	Doi Malingri	DNF
Vivanapoli	Italy	Beppe Panada	DNF
Scandinavian	Sweden	Reino Engqvist	DNF
Swedish Entry	Sweden	Peder Sifverheim	DNF
Bubblegum	UK	Ian McGowan-Fyfe	DNF

THE ROUTE		DISTANCE 26,095 NM
Leg 1	Portsmouth to Cape Town	Start 29 Aug 1981
Leg 2	Cape Town to Auckland	Restart 31 Oct 1981
Leg 3	Auckland to Mar del Plata	Restart 26 Dec 1981
Leg 4	Mar del Plata to Portsmouth	Restart 27 Feb 1982

1.	L'Esprit d'Equipe	France	Lionel Péan	
2.	Philips Innovator	Netherlands	Dirk Nauta	
3.	Fazer Finland	Finland	Michael Berner	
4.	UBS Switzerland	Switzerland	Pierre Fehlmann	
5.	Rucanor Tristar	Belgium	Gustaf Versluys	
			Ann Lippens	
6.	Fortuna Lights	Spain	Javier Visiers	
			Jorgie Brufau	
			Antonio Guiu	
7.	Lion New Zealand	New Zealand	Peter Blake	
8.	Drum	UK	Skip Novak	
9.	Equity & Law	Netherlands	Pleun van der Lugt	
10.	Côte d'Or	Belgium	Eric Tabarly	
11.	Shadow of Switzerland	Switzerland	Otto & Nora	
			Zehender-Mueller	
12.	Norsk Data GB	UK	Bob Salmon	
13.	SAS Baia Viking	Denmark	Jesper Norsk	
NZI Enterprise		New Zealand	Digby Taylor	DNF
Atlantic Privateer		USA	Padda Kuttel	DNF

THE ROUTE		DISTANCE 26,740 NM
Leg 1	Portsmouth to Cape Town	Start 28 Sep 1985
Leg 2	Cape Town to Auckland	Restart 4 Dec 1985
Leg 3	Auckland to Punta del Este	Restart 14 Feb 1986
Leg 4	Punta del Este to Portsmouth	Restart 9 Apr 1986

1.	Steinlager 2	New Zealand	Peter Blake
2.	Fisher & Paykel	New Zealand	Grant Dalton
3.	Merit	Switzerland	Pierre Fehlmann
4.	Rothmans	UK	Lawrie Smith
5.	The Card	Sweden	Roger Nilson
6.	Charles Jourdan	France	Alain Gabbay
7.	Fortuna Extra Lights	Spain	Javier de la Gaudera
			Jan Santana
			José Luis Doreste
8.	Gatorade	Italy	Giorgio Falck
			Hervé Jan
			Perre Sicouri
9.	Union Bank of Finland	Finland	Ludde Ingvall
10.	Belmont Finland II	Finland	Harry Harkimo
11.	Fazisi	USSR	Alexi Grischenko
			Skip Novak
			Valeri Alexeev
12.	NCB Ireland	Ireland	Joe English
13.	British Satquote Defender	UK	Frank Esson
			Colin Watkins
14.	Equity and Law II	Netherlands	Dirk Nauta
15.	Liverpool Enterprise	UK	Bob Salmon
16.	Creighton's Naturally	UK	John Chittenden
17.	Esprit de Liberté	France	Patrick Tabarly
18.	Maiden	UK	Tracy Edwards
19.	Schlussel von Bremen	Germany	Rolf Renken
			Ham Müeller-Röhlok
			Jochen Orgelmann
			Wilhelm-Otto Beck
			Peter Weidner
20.	With Integrity	UK	Andy Coghill
21.	La Poste	France	Daniel Mallé
Rucanor Sport		Belgium	Bruno Dubois	DNF
Martela OF		Finland	Markku Wilkeri	DNF

THE ROUTE		DISTANCE 32,000 NM
Leg 1	Southampton to Punta del Este	Start 2 Sep 1989
Leg 2	Punta Del Este to Fremantle	Restart 28 Oct 1989
Leg 3	Fremantle to Auckland	Restart 23 Dec 1989
Leg 4	Auckland to Punta del Este	Restart 4 Feb 1990
Leg 5	Punta del Este to Fort Lauderdale	Restart 17 Mar 1990
Leg 6	Fort Lauderdale to Southampton	Restart 5 May 1990

MAXI CLASS

1.	NZ Endeavour	New Zealand	Grant Dalton
2.	Merit Cup	Switzerland	Pierre Fehlmann
3.	La Poste	France	Eric Tabarly
4.	Uruguay Natural	Uruguay	Gustavo Vanzini

WHITBREAD 60 CLASS

1.	Yamaha	Japan	Ross Field
2.	Intrum Justitia	Europe	Lawrie Smith
3.	Galicia '93 Pescanova	Spain	Javier Gandara
4.	Winston	USA	Dennis Conner
			Brad Butterworth
5.	Tokio	Japan	Chris Dickson
6.	Brooksfield	Italy	Guido Maisto
7.	Hetman Sahaidachny	Ukraine	Eugene Platon
8.	Dolphin & Youth	UK	Matt Humphries
9.	Heineken	USA	Dawn Riley
10.	Odessa	Ukraine	Anatoly Verba

THE ROUTE		DISTANCE 32,000 NM
Leg 1	Southampton to Punta del Este	Start 25 Sep 1993
Leg 2	Punta Del Este to Fremantle	Restart 13 Nov 1993
Leg 3	Fremantle to Auckland	Restart 9 Jan 1994
Leg 4	Auckland to Punta del Este	Restart 20 Feb 1994
Leg 5	Punta del Este to Fort Lauderdale	Restart 2 Apr 1994
Leg 6	Fort Lauderdale to Southampton	Restart 21 May 1994

RACE SEVEN 1997–98

1.	EF Language	Sweden	Paul Cayard
2.	Merit Cup	Monaco	Grant Dalton
3.	Swedish Match	Sweden	Gunnar Krantz
4.	Innovation Kvaerner	Norway	Knut Frostad
5.	Silk Cut	UK	Lawrie Smith
6.	Chessie Racing	USA	George Collins
7.	Toshiba	USA	Dennis Conner
			Paul Standbridge
8.	BrunelSunergy	Netherlands	Hans Bouscholte
			Roy Heiner
9.	EF Education	Sweden	Christine Guillou

America's Challenge		USA	Ross Field DNF

THE ROUTE — DISTANCE 31,600 NM

Leg 1	Southampton to Cape Town	Start 21 Sept 1997
Leg 2	Cape Town to Fremantle	Restart 11 Nov 1997
Leg 3	Fremantle to Sydney	Restart 13 Dec 1997
Leg 4	Sydney to Auckland	Restart 4 Jan 1998
Leg 5	Auckland to São Sebastião	Restart 1 Feb 1998
Leg 6	São Sebastião to Fort Lauderdale	Restart 14 Mar 1998
Leg 7	Fort Lauderdale to Baltimore	Restart 19 Apr 1998
Leg 8	Baltimore/Annapolis to La Rochelle	Restart 3 May 1998
Leg 9	La Rochelle to Southampton	Restart 22 May 1998

RACE EIGHT 2001–02

1.	illbruck	USA	John Kostecki
2.	ASSA ABLOY	Sweden	Neal McDonald
3.	Amer Sports One	New Zealand	Grant Dalton
4.	Tyco	USA	Kevin Shoebridge
5.	News Corp	New Zealand	Jez Fanstone
6.	djuice	Norway	Knut Frostad
7.	SEB	Sweden	Gunnar Krantz
8.	Amer Sports Too	USA/UK	Lisa McDonald

THE ROUTE — DISTANCE 32,250 NM

Leg 1	Southampton to Cape Town	Start 23 Sep 2001
Leg 2	Cape Town to Sydney	Restart 11 Nov 2001
Leg 3	Sydney to Auckland	Restart 26 Dec 2001
Leg 4	Auckland to Rio de Janeiro	Restart 27 Jan 2002
Leg 5	Rio de Janeiro to Miami	Restart 09 Mar 2002
Leg 6	Miami to Baltimore	Restart 14 Apr 2002
Leg 7	Baltimore/Annapolis to La Rochelle	Restart 28 Apr 2002
Leg 8	La Rochelle to Göteborg	Restart 25 May 2002
Leg 9	Göteborg to Kiel	Restart 06 Jun 2002

RACE NINE 2005–06

1.	ABN AMRO ONE	Netherlands	Mike Sanderson
2.	Pirates of the Caribbean	USA	Paul Cayard
3.	Brasil 1	Brazil	Torben Grael
4.	ABN AMRO TWO	Netherlands	Sébastien Josse
5.	Ericsson	Sweden	Neal McDonald
6.	movistar	Spain	Bouwe Bekking
7.	Brunel	Netherlands	Matt Humphries

THE ROUTE — DISTANCE 31,250 NM

In-Port Race 1 Sanxenxo	5 Nov 2005
Leg 1 Vigo to Cape Town	Start 12 Nov 2005
In-Port Race 2 Cape Town	26 Dec 2005
Leg 2 Cape Town to Melbourne	Restart 2 Jan 2006
In-Port Race 3 Melbourne	4 Feb 2006
Leg 3 Melbourne to Wellington	Restart 12 Feb 2006
Leg 4 Wellington to Rio de Janeiro	Restart 19 Feb 2006
In-Port Race 4 Rio de Janeiro	25 Mar 2006
Leg 5 Rio de Janeiro to Baltimore	Restart 2 Apr 2006
In-Port Race 5 Baltimore	29 Apr 2006
Leg 6 Baltimore/Annapolis to New York	Restart 7 May 2006
Leg 7 New York to Portsmouth	Restart 11 May 2006
In-Port Race 6 Portsmouth	29 May 2006
Leg 8 Portsmouth to Rotterdam	Restart 2 Jun 2006
In-Port Race 7 Rotterdam	11 Jun 2006
Leg 9 Rotterdam to Göteborg	Restart 15 Jun 2006

Crew List 2008–09

DATE OF BIRTH		CREW LIST (OFFSHORE LEGS ONLY)	LEG 1	LEG 2	LEG 3	LEG 4	LEG 5	LEG 6	LEG 7	LEG 8	LEG 9	LEG 10
		DELTA LLOYD					DNS					
17.11.61	1	Ger O'Rourke/IRL – skipper	●									
18.10.76	2	Matthew Gregory/USA – navigator	●	●	●							
07.02.84	3	Sander Pluijm/NED – media crew member	●	●	●	●		●	●	●	●	●
10.12.66	4	Stuart Wilson/NZL – watch captain	●	●	●			●	●	●		●
29.07.82	5	Stuart Molloy/NZL – watch captain	●									
23.02.80	6	Edwin O'Connor/IRL – trimmer/helmsman	●	●	●							
28.04.80	7	Martin Watts/GBR – trimmer/helmsman	●	●	●	●						
06.10.82	8	Ryan Houston/NZL – helmsman/watch captain	●	●	●							
01.05.83	9	Bert Schandevyl/BEL – trimmer/helmsman	●									
03.05.76	10	Gerd-Jan Poortman/NED – bowman	●	●	●			●	●	●	●	●
11.06.75	11	Eduard van Lierde/NED – trimmer/helmsman	●	●	●			●	●	●	●	●
01.03.70	12	Roberto Bérmudez de Castro/ESP – skipper		●	●	●		●	●	●	●	●
30.11.71	13	Peter Van Nierkerk/NED – helmsman		●	●							
01.12.84	14	Morgan White/AUS – bowman		●	●	●		●	●	●		●
24.03.55	15	Fritz Koek/NED – navigator				●						
15.06.62	16	Guillermo Altadill/ESP – watch captain				●						
08.08.78	17	Andre Fonseca/BRA – helmsman				●		●	●	●	●	●
27.03.71	18	David Pella/ESP – trimmer/pitman				●		●	●	●	●	●
16.11.75	19	Wouter Verbraak/NED – navigator						●	●	●	●	●
17.06.79	20	Ben Costello/NZL – helmsman						●	●	●	●	●
19.01.78	21	Nick Bice/AUS – watch captain						●	●	●	●	●
		ERICSSON 4										
22.07.60	1	Torben Grael/BRA – skipper	●	●	●	●	●	●	●	●	●	●
18.12.68	2	Jules Salter/GBR – navigator	●	●	●	●	●	●	●	●	●	●
05.03.72	3	Guy Salter/GBR – media crew member	●	●	●	●	●	●	●	●	●	●
05.04.68	4	Brad Jackson/NZL – watch captain	●	●	●	●	●	●	●	●	●	●
20.04.71	5	Stu Bannatyne/NZL – watch captain	●	●	●	●	●	●	●	●	●	●
30.10.77	6	David Endean/NZL – pitman	●	●	●	●	●	●	●	●	●	●
10.02.68	7	Horacio Carabelli/BRA – trimmer	●	●	●	●	●	●	●	●	●	●
17.01.69	8	Tony Mutter/NZL – trimmer	●	●	●	●	●	●	●	●	●	●
22.07.77	9	João Signorini/BRA – trimmer	●	●	●	●	●	●	●	●	●	●
10.10.80	10	Ryan Godfrey/AUS – bowman	●	●	●	●	●	●	●	●	●	●
30.07.77	11	Phil Jameson/NZL – bowman	●	●	●	●	●	●	●	●	●	●
		ERICSSON 3										
02.11.63	1	Anders Lewander/SWE – skipper	●	●	●							
06.03.79	2	Aksel Magdahl/NOR – navigator	●	●	●	●	●	●	●	●	●	●
01.02.84	3	Gustav Morin/SWE – media crew member	●	●	●		●	●	●	●		●
28.06.74	4	Richard Mason/NZL – watch captain	●	●	●	●	●	●	●	●		●
04.01.49	5	Magnus Olsson/SWE – watch captain/skipper	●	●	●	●	●	●	●	●		●
03.06.69	6	Thomas Johanson/FIN – helmsman	●	●	●	●	●	●	●	●		●
19.04.72	7	Eivind Melleby/NOR – helmsman	●	●	●		●	●	●		●	●
27.10.59	8	Stefan Myrälf/DEN – trimmer	●									
23.05.69	9	Jens Dolmer/DEN – pitman	●	●	●		●	●	●	●		●
28.06.72	10	Anders Dahlsjö/SWE – mastman	●	●	●		●	●	●	●		●
08.12.80	11	Martin Krite/SWE – bowman	●	●	●		●	●	●	●		●
03.04.82	12	Martin Strömberg/SWE – trimmer		●	●		●	●	●	●		●
24.09.66	13	Klas Nylöf/SWE – helmsman				●						
16.12.63	14	Jann Neergaard/DEN – pitman				●						
07.05.62	15	Arve Roaas/NOR – helmsman/trimmer					●	●	●	●	●	●
27.04.71	16	Magnus Woxén/SWE – helmsman/trimmer					●	●		●		

DATE OF BIRTH		CREW LIST (OFFSHORE LEGS ONLY)	LEG 1	LEG 2	LEG 3	LEG 4	LEG 5	LEG 6	LEG 7	LEG 8	LEG 9	LEG 10
		GREEN DRAGON										
25.02.70	1	Ian Walker/GBR – skipper	•	•	•	•	•	•	•	•	•	•
25.03.71	2	Ian Moore/IRL – navigator	•	•		•		•	•	•	•	
05.01.65	3	Guo Chuan/CHN – media crew member	•	•	•	•	•	•	•			•
07.03.69	4	Damian Foxall/IRL – watch captain	•	•	•		•	•	•		•	•
22.07.63	5	Neal McDonald/GBR – watch captain	•	•	•	•		•	•	•	•	•
08.01.73	6	Anthony Merrington/AUS – helmsman/trimmer	•	•	•	•		•	•	•	•	•
26.06.79	7	Phil Harmer/AUS – helmsman/trimmer	•	•	•		•	•	•	•	•	•
13.03.72	8	Tom Braidwood/AUS – pitman/trimmer	•	•	•	•	•	•	•	•	•	•
06.09.79	9	Andrew McLean/NZL – pitman/trimmer	•	•	•	•	•	•	•	•	•	
18.04.80	10	Freddie Shanks/GBR – bowman	•	•	•	•	•	•	•	•	•	
08.07.74	11	Justin Slattery/IRL – bowman	•	•	•	•	•	•	•	•	•	
23.02.73	12	Steve Hayles/GBR – navigator			•			•		•		•
18.02.77	13	James Carroll/IRL – pitman			•			•				•
30.06.70	14	Ian Budgen/GBR – helmsman/trimmer					•		•			•
16.11.75	15	Wouter Verbraak/NED – navigator					•					
02.10.74	16	Chris Main/NZL – helmsman/trimmer					•					
30.05.71	17	Huang Jian/CHN – media crew member									•	
08.06.62	18	Jean-Luc Nelias/FRA – navigator										•
		PUMA										
24.01.61	1	Ken Read/USA – skipper	•	•	•	•	•	•	•	•	•	•
28.06.62	2	Andrew Cape/AUS – navigator	•	•	•	•	•	•	•	•		•
11.07.64	3	Rick Deppe/GBR – media crew member	•	•	•	•	•	•	•	•		•
23.12.68	4	Sidney Gavignet/FRA – watch captain	•	•	•	•	•	•				
18.06.69	5	Chris Nicholson/AUS – watch captain	•	•	•							
13.01.83	6	Michael Müeller/GER – helmsman/trimmer	•	•	•	•	•	•	•	•		•
05.12.65	7	Rob Salthouse/NZL – helmsman/trimmer	•	•	•	•	•	•	•			•
12.10.78	8	Casey Smith/AUS – bowman	•	•	•	•	•	•	•	•	•	•
12.05.56	9	Jerry Kirby/USA – bowman	•				•					•
19.12.59	10	Jonathan McKee/USA – helmsman/trimmer	•									
12.05.75	11	Justin Ferris/NZL – helmsman/trimmer	•	•	•	•	•	•	•	•	•	
04.05.64	12	Robbie Naismith/NZL – helmsman/trimmer		•								
28.06.81	13	Shannon Falcone/ANT – trimmer/pitman		•	•	•		•				•
17.08.77	14	Robert Greenhalgh/GBR – helmsman/watch captain				•	•	•	•	•	•	•
13.10.58	15	Erle Williams/NZL – watch captain					•	•	•	•	•	•
23.09.73	16	Craig Satterthwaite/NZL – helmsman/trimmer							•	•	•	•
		TEAM RUSSIA				DNS	DNS	DNS	DNS	DNS	DNS	DNS
01.07.66	1	Andreas Hanakamp/AUT – skipper	•	•	•							
16.11.75	2	Wouter Verbraak/NED – navigator	•	•	•							
07.11.67	3	Mark Covell/GBR – media crew member	•	•								
16.09.63	4	Stig Westergaard/DEN – watch captain	•	•	•							
15.06.63	5	Guillermo Altadill/ESP – watch captain	•									
29.10.72	6	Rodion Luka/UKR – helmsman	•	•	•							
21.03.79	7	Jeremy Elliott/IRL – trimmer	•	•	•							
17.06.79	8	Ben Costello/NZL – trimmer	•	•	•							
05.02.72	9	Mike Joubert/RSA – bowman	•	•	•							
01.04.79	10	Nick Bubb/GBR – trimmer/watch captain	•	•	•							
26.07.77	11	Cameron Wills/RSA – pitman	•	•	•							
21.05.68	12	Oleg Zherebtsov/RUS – bowman		•								
10.09.63	13	Sergey Bogdanov/RUS – media crew member			•							
19.01.82	14	Scott Gray/GBR – bowman/pitman			•							

DATE OF BIRTH		CREW LIST (OFFSHORE LEGS ONLY)	LEG 1	LEG 2	LEG 3	LEG 4	LEG 5	LEG 6	LEG 7	LEG 8	LEG 9	LEG 10
		TELEFÓNICA BLUE										
17.06.63	1	Bouwe Bekking/NED – skipper	•	•	•	•	•	•	•	•	•	•
16.06.77	2	Iker Martínez/ESP – co-skipper/helmsman	•	•	•	•	•	•	•	•	•	•
20.01.78	3	Simon Fisher/GBR – navigator/strategist	•	•	•	•	•	•			•	•
31.03.78	4	Gabriele Olivo/ITA – media crew member	•	•	•	•	•	•	•	•	•	•
27.01.67	5	Jonathan Swain/RSA – watch captain	•	•	•	•	•	•	•	•	•	•
20.10.76	6	Laurent Pages/FRA – helmsman	•	•	•	•	•	•	•	•	•	•
24.06.68	7	Jordi Calafat/ESP – helmsman	•	•	•	•	•	•	•	•	•	•
19.10.76	8	Xabier Fernández/ESP – trimmer	•	•	•	•	•	•	•	•	•	•
11.11.80	9	Pablo Arrarte/ESP – trimmer	•	•	•	•	•	•	•	•	•	•
20.05.81	10	Daryl Wislang/NZL – bowman	•	•	•	•	•	•	•	•	•	•
19.06.71	11	Pepe Ribes/ESP – bowman	•		•		•	•	•	•	•	•
01.03.70	12	Tom Addis/AUS – navigator			•		•	•	•	•		
19.07.70	13	David Vera/ESP – bowman					•					
11.03.83	14	Michael Pammenter/RSA – bowman					•					
		TELEFÓNICA BLACK					DNS					
13.08.72	1	Fernando Echávarri/ESP – skipper	•	•	•	•		•	•	•	•	•
05.03.49	2	Roger Nilson/SWE – navigator	•	•	•			•	•	•		
20.10.66	3	Mikel Pasabant/ESP – media crew member	•	•	•	•						
22.09.61	4	Santiago Lange/ARG – watch captain	•	•	•							
24.04.72	5	Jaime Arbones/ESP – watch captain	•	•				•	•	•	•	•
24.09.73	6	Maciel Cicchetti/ARG – trimmer	•					•	•	•	•	•
22.10.73	7	Javier de la Plaza/ESP – trimmer/helmsman	•	•	•	•		•	•	•	•	•
19.07.70	8	David Vera/ESP – trimmer	•	•	•	•		•	•	•	•	•
22.12.81	9	Antonio Cuervas-Mons/ESP – bowman	•	•	•	•		•	•	•		
22.10.63	10	Francisco Rivero/ESP – bowman	•									
11.03.83	11	Michael Pammenter/RSA – bowman	•	•	•			•	•	•	•	•
26.02.69	12	Gonzalo Araujo/ESP – watch captain		•	•			•	•	•		
07.06.69	13	Pablo Iglesias/ESP – trimmer/helmsman		•	•			•	•	•	•	•
08.08.76	14	Anton Paz/ESP – media crew member						•	•	•	•	•

Prize Winners 2008–09

Leg One   Alicante – Cape Town
1. Ericsson 4
2. PUMA
3. Green Dragon

24-hour run: Ericsson 4 – 596.6 nm
Inmarsat Media Prize: Guy Salter/Ericsson 4
Wallenius Wilhelmsen Logistics Seamanship Award:
   Martin Watts/Delta Lloyd

Leg Two   Cape Town – Cochin
1. Ericsson 4
2. Telefónica Blue
3. Ericsson 3

24-hour run: Ericsson 4 – 522.0 nm
Inmarsat Media Prize: Gabriele Olivo/Telefónica Blue
Wallenius Wilhelmsen Logistics Seamanship Award:
   Green Dragon Team

Leg Three   Cochin – Singapore
1. Telefónica Blue
2. PUMA
3. Ericsson 3

24-hour run: Team Russia 293.2 nm
Inmarsat Media Prize: Rick Deppe/PUMA
Wallenius Wilhelmsen Logistics Seamanship Award:
   Edwin O'Connor/Delta Lloyd

Leg Four   Singapore – Qingdao
1. Telefónica Blue
2. PUMA
3. Ericsson 4

24-hour run: Ericsson 3 – 334.5 nm
Inmarsat Media Prize: Rick Deppe/PUMA
Wallenius Wilhelmsen Logistics Seamanship Award:
   Green Dragon Team

Leg Five   Qingdao – Rio de Janeiro
1. Ericsson 3
2. Ericsson 4
3. PUMA

24-hour run: Ericsson 3 – 547.3 nm
Inmarsat Media Prize: Gustav Morin/Ericsson 3
Wallenius Wilhelmsen Logistics Seamanship Award:
   David Vera/Telefónica Blue
Roaring 40s Trophy: Ericsson 4

Leg Six   Rio de Janeiro – Boston
1. Ericsson 4
2. Ericsson 3
3. Telefónica Blue

24-hour run: PUMA – 497.6 nm
Inmarsat Media Prize: Gustav Morin/Ericsson 3
Wallenius Wilhelmsen Logistics Seamanship Award:
   Nick Bice/Delta Lloyd

Leg Seven   Boston – Galway
1. Ericsson 4
2. PUMA
3. Green Dragon

24-hour run: Ericsson 4 – 539.5 nm
Inmarsat Media Prize: Rick Deppe/PUMA
Wallenius Wilhelmsen Logistics Seamanship Award:
   Casey Smith/PUMA

Leg Eight   Galway – Göteborg (Marstrand)
1. Ericsson 4
2. PUMA
3. Green Dragon

24-hour run: Green Dragon – 329.5 nm
Inmarsat Media Prize: Gabriele Olivo/Telefónica Blue
Wallenius Wilhelmsen Logistics Seamanship Award:
   Pablo Arrarte/Telefónica Blue

Leg Nine   Göteborg (Marstrand) – Stockholm
1. PUMA
2. Ericsson 3
3. Ericsson 4

24-hour run: Telefónica Blue – 312.0 nm
Inmarsat Media Prize: Gabriele Olivo/Telefónica Blue
Wallenius Wilhelmsen Logistics Seamanship Award:
   PUMA shore crew

Leg Ten   Stockholm – St Petersburg
1. Telefónica Black
2. PUMA
3. Telefónica Blue

24-hour run: PUMA – 242.79 nm
Inmarsat Media Prize: Rick Deppe/PUMA
Wallenius Wilhelmsen Logistics Seamanship Award:
   Not awarded

Overall
1. Ericsson 4
2. PUMA
3. Telefónica Blue
4. Ericsson 3
5. Green Dragon
6. Telefónica Black
7. Delta Lloyd
8. Team Russia

Hans Horrevoets Rookie Award: Michi Müeller/PUMA
Overall Best 24-hour run: Ericsson 4 – 596.6 nm
Overall Inmarsat Media Prize: Rick Deppe/PUMA
Overall Wallenius Wilhelmsen Logistics Seamanship
   Award: PUMA shore crew
In-Shore Series Winner: Telefónica Blue
Virtual Race Winner: Hugo Zwaal
Virtual Race Top Lady Competitor: Linde van de Wal

Alicante In-Port Race
1. Telefónica Blue
2. Telefónica Black
3. PUMA

Singapore In-Port Race
1. Ericsson 4
2. PUMA
3. Telefónica Blue

Qingdao In-Port Race
1. Ericsson 4
2. Telefónica Blue
3. PUMA

Rio de Janeiro In-Port Race
1. Telefónica Blue
2. PUMA
3. Delta Lloyd

Boston In-Port Race
1. Telefónica Blue
2. Ericsson 4
3. Delta Lloyd

Galway In-Port Race
1. PUMA
2. Telefónica Blue
3. Telefónica Black

Stockholm In-Port Race
1. Telefónica Blue
2. PUMA
3. Telefónica Black

How the points were won

	Delta Lloyd	Ericsson 3	Ericsson 4	Green Dragon	PUMA	Team Russia	Telefónica Blue	Telefónica Black
Overall position	7	4	1	5	2	8	3	6
Total points	41.5	78.5	114.5	67	105.5	10.5	98***	58***
In-Port Race Alicante	1	0.5*	2.5	2	3	0.5	4	3.5
Scoring Gate Fernando de Noronha	1	0.5*	3.5	4	3	0.5	2	2.5
Leg One	2	4**	8	5	7	3	4	1
Scoring Gate 58 deg E	0.5	3.5	4	3	1	2.5	2	1.5
Leg Two	3	6	8	2	4	1	7	5
Scoring Gate Pulau We	0.5	3	4	1.5	2.5	1	3.5	2
Leg Three	1	5*	5	3	7	2	8	4
In-Port Race Singapore	1	1.5	4	2	3.5	DNS	3	2.5
Leg Four	2 DNF	4	6	5	7	DNS	8	2 DNF
In-Port Race Qingdao	DNS	DNS	4	2.5	3	DNS	3.5	DNS
Scoring Gate 36 deg S	-	3.5	4	2	3	-	2.5	-
Scoring Gate Cape Horn	-	4	3.5	2.5	3	-	2	-
Leg Five	DNS	8	7	5	6	DNS	4	DNS
In-Port Race Rio de Janeiro	3	1	2.5	1.5	3.5	-	4	2
Scoring Gate Fernando de Noronha	3	1.5	3.5	1	2.5	DNS	4	2
Leg Six	3	7	8	2	5	DNS	6	4
In-Port Race Boston	3	2.5	3.5	1	1.5	DNS	4	2
Scoring Gate St John's	1.5	2.5	3	1	3.5	-	4	2
Leg Seven	4	2	8	6	7	DNS	5	3
In-Port Race Galway	1.5	2.5	2	1	4	-	3.5	3
Leg Eight	4	2	8	6	7	DNS	5	3
Leg Nine	3	7	6	4	8	DNS	2	5
In-Port Race Stockholm	1.5	2	2.5	1	3.5	DNS	4	3
Leg Ten	2	5	4	3	7	DNS	6	8

Key

DNS Did not start
DNF Did not finish

* 1 penalty point deducted
** 2 penalty points deducted
*** 3 penalty points deducted for rudder change

First Place
Second Place
Third Place

Scoring system

The Volvo Ocean Race used a high-scoring system: with eight entries, eight points were awarded to the winner of each leg, seven points for second, and so on.
The scoring gates used on the longer legs, and the in-port racing, both offered half points: four points for the winner, 3.5 for second, and so on.
The overall winner was the team with the most points at the end of the race.

SCORING GATES

1. Fernando de Noronha
2. Mauritius
3. Pulau We, Indonesia
4. Latitude 36°S
5. Cape Horn
6. Fernando de Noron
7. St John's, Newfoun

GEOGRAPHICAL REFER

A Cape Verde Island
B Sri Lanka
C Spratly Islands
D Taiwan and Luzo
E Fiji
F Cabo Frio
G Nova Scotia
H Alderney
I Skagerrak
J Öresund
K Öland

GALWAY

7

H

BOSTON

G

ALICANTE

A

1

6

F

RIO DE JANEIRO

4